Joplinites were filled with civic goodwill during the Roaring Twenties and many clubs held fund-raising activities. This parade down Main Street was sponsored by the Shrine Club. Courtesy, Dorothea B. Hoover Historical Museum

5

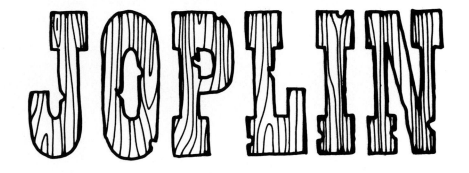

This is a circa 1915 view of Joplin's Main Street looking north from Seventh. The two large structures in the foreground are Newman's Department Store (left) and the Frisco building (right). Both edifices are still standing. In the distant background are the Connor and Keystone hotels on the left and right respectively. Both have now been razed. Courtesy, Ron Mosbaugh

JOPLIN

FROM MINING TOWN TO URBAN CENTER

An Illustrated History by G.K. Renner

"PARTNERS IN PROGRESS" BY PHILIP L. JONES

PRODUCED IN COOPERATION WITH
THE JOPLIN HISTORICAL SOCIETY

WINDSOR PUBLICATIONS, INC.
NORTHRIDGE, CALIFORNIA

Windsor Publications, Inc. — History Book Division
Publisher: John M. Phillips
Editorial Director: Teri Davis Greenberg
Design Director: Alexander D'Anca

Staff for *Joplin: From Mining Town to Urban Center*
Senior Editor: Nancy Evans
Director, Corporate Biographies: Karen Story
Assistant Director, Corporate Biographies: Phyllis Gray
Editor, Corporate Biographies: Judith Hunter
Proofreader: Jerry Mosher
Editorial Assistants: Kathy M. Brown, Patricia Cobb, Lonnie Pham,
    Pat Pittman, Deena Tucker

Picture Researcher: Mark Spangler
Research Assistant: Peter Shanafelt

Advisory Committee
Kerri Johnston
Michael Gilpin
Rolla Stephens
Dr. Julio Leon
Burleigh DeTar
Joy Spiva Cragin
David Patrick
Jack Fleischaker
William Perry III
Penny Thompson

Library of Congress Cataloging in Publication Data

Renner, G. K. (Gail K.), 1924-
    Joplin: from mining town to urban center.

    "Produced in cooperation with the Joplin Historical Society."
    Bibliography: p.
    Includes index.
    1. Joplin (Mo.)—History. 2. Joplin (Mo.)—Description. 3. Joplin
(Mo.)—Industries. I. Jones, Philip L. II. Joplin Historical Society. III.
Title.
F474.J8R46 1985   977.8'72   85-9341
ISBN 0-89781-153-4

CONTENTS

TO NICKEY

PREFACE

Writing a history of Joplin is an enriching experience. Few cities of its size or comparative youth have had such an eventful past. To delve into the many facets of its history makes a researcher more appreciative of the city in which he lives. Much of that story cannot be included in this short volume, but a rich opportunity awaits any writer who wants to dig deeper into Joplin's past.

Much has been written on Joplin's history, but most of these accounts deal only with particular episodes or colorful anecdotes. Furthermore, there exists no comprehensive account of the last seventy-five years. The writings we have on this period are fragmentary. They deal in particular with topics such as mining or civic development, or they are vignettes of Joplinites who have captured the public spotlight.

The standard accounts of Joplin's earlier history are *History of Jasper County, Missouri*, edited by F.A. North, and *A History of Jasper County, Missouri, and Its People*, by Joel T. Livingston. These comprehensive county histories give fairly complete accounts of Joplin, but North's story ends in 1880 and Livingston carried the narrative only to 1910. These books are sound works of scholarship. Both North and Livingston researched old newspaper files and other written records, and they also drew on the reminiscences of pioneers, many of whom were instrumental in founding Joplin and the mining industry. In the latter respect, both works are indispensable resources. Later writings dwell heavily on the colorful period covered so well by North and Livingston, to the neglect of later decades.

This brief narrative attempts to present a balanced account of Joplin's development up to the 1980s. A central theme of this work is how Joplin has evolved from a raw mining boomtown to an urban center that serves as a manufacturing, wholesale, retail, cultural, transportation, and medical services hub for the Four-State district of southwest Missouri, southeast Kansas, northeast Oklahoma, and northwest Arkansas. A secondary theme is how the mining industry provided a vital thrust to Joplin's development in the first eighty years of its existence.

The mining industry favored Joplin more than most towns that sprang from such origins. Mining is an extractive industry that lends itself to exploitation. The world offers many examples of abandoned mine fields where the wealth has been siphoned off along with the ore, leaving behind a legacy of environmental blight and impoverished, declining towns. The Tri-State zinc and lead industry treated Joplin more kindly—more favorably, in fact, than it did other district towns. Wealth produced by Tri-State zinc and lead did indeed flow out of the district, but much also flowed into Joplin. Emerging as the district's capital, Joplin became the administrative and financial center of the Tri-State mining fields. The manufacture of specialized mining machinery also centered here, and as the city developed, railroads built to it. Governmental policies favored Joplin with national highway connections that greatly augmented its emerging role as a district center, and public policies favored the city with airport facilities and television stations that further solidified its regional role. The stream of mineral wealth also enabled Joplin to build a strong structure of municipal services, progressive schools, and cultural centers that have furthered the city's development.

I am very thankful for the support extended in this undertaking. Since the project's announcement, many people have called to lend encouragement and to provide bits of information. Space does not permit me to mention all these individuals, but I am nonetheless grateful.

I especially want to acknowledge those people who have provided a rich fund of information through lengthy interviews. Lee Dagley, drawing on the vivid memories of his ninety-five years in Joplin, provided a wealth of information about life in early Joplin and about the mining industry. Rolla Stephens, recalling his sixty-year career as a leading realtor, provided invaluable information about business in the city as well as letting me share in the use of his own writings and his collection of historical photos. Vernon Sigars drew on memories of his active fifty-year career in business and public affairs to provide many insights and also lent the use of his photos. Marvin Van Filder clarified my research on early Jasper County and on Annie Baxter. Colleen Belk, a leading authority on local genealogy and old cemeteries, pointed out discrepancies in earlier accounts of the Joplin family and provided new insights into the movement of pioneer families into the Joplin area. Thelma Meeks provided information on the city's black community that could not be obtained from written sources. Jack Karch recalled in wonderful detail the Joplin he grew up in more than a half-century ago. Bruce Quisenberry provided a copy of his excellent account of Joplin's history. Thomas J. Cusack gave new perspectives on the business community in the early post-World War II period, and Jim Lobbey reminisced about the early days of television. Lou Martin of KOAM-TV, Bill Clark of KSNF-TV, and Gail Kirchner of KODE-TV also gave information on early-day television, and Mrs. Kirchner provided photos. I am also grateful to former mayor, Lena Beal, for the use of her picture and to Virginia Wieda for information about her mother's kindergarten and for the use of a photo.

A number of people and organizations who helped research this project deserve special recognition. Mark Spangler cheerfully spent many hours selecting photos for the book and in the research and writing of captions. Peter Shanafelt did laudatory work in researching microfilm records for the project and in gathering information through interviews. Philip Jones, the editorial consultant and author of the business biographies, has generously worked with me and related accounts of his own rich background in the mining history of Joplin. The Joplin Historical Society, sponsor of this project, has been truly supportive. Helen Chickering, president; Sue Gardner, past president; Barbara Hicklin, Mary Louise Wagner, Philip Jones, Mark Spangler, and other members of the board of directors have been very cooperative in promoting and supporting the undertaking.

Other individuals and organizations also deserve special thanks. The late Darral Dishman went out of his way to assemble a collection of paintings for inclusion in the book. The Tri-State Mineral Museum made available their extensive collection of photos and research material. The Joplin Globe Publishing Company has supported the project and William Caldwell, the *Globe's* librarian, has been unfailingly friendly and helpful in responding to my endless inquiries. Missouri Southern State College has also strongly supported the project with a biography and the use of their facilities. Mary Lou Dove, head librarian; Carolyn Trout, circulation librarian; and other members of the MSSC library staff have been unceasingly cooperative in making research materials available. Gwen Hunt, MSSC's director of public information, has enthusiastically gathered photos and information on the early history of the college. The Joplin Public Library has found me to be one of their most persistent patrons in recent months. Joan Banks, head librarian, and her staff have been consistently helpful. I especially wish to thank Norma Rainwater, Vincent Travis, Earl Long, Betty Baker, and Ailene Hubbard of the Joplin Genealogical Society who have courteously helped me during months of research. Credit is also due the State Historical Society of Missouri. James W. Goodrich, Leona S. Morris, and other members of the staff were always friendly and cooperative in making the society's vast collection of photos and research materials available.

I also wish to thank Windsor Publications who made this book possible. Nancy Evans, the editor, has been most understanding, patient, and helpful through the long months of this book's incubation. Finally, I wish to thank my wife, Nickey, who has strongly supported the project with her faith, patience, and hard work.

Any errors are my own. *G.K.R.*

INTRODUCTION

There is always need to write a new history because every new one freshens the past and relates it with a little more relevance to the present.

The Joplin Historical Society believed this should be their concern, because no general history of Joplin was available. Of the excellent books on Joplin, most were concerned with personalities of the old days and others depended on illustrations. Therefore an orthodox treatment of Joplin history coordinating all aspects of its development: environmental, social, economic, industrial, religious, educational, and recreational, all brought up to the present, was due. This is a tall order but this book is an attempt to fulfill these aspects in the available space.

Joplin is a unique town with a unique history. It was founded in a beautiful country which did not have the navigable rivers or well-traveled crossroads that usually gave rise to large settlements. Joplin was founded in 1873 on the mining of lead and zinc, and very little else. For thirty years, zinc was king.

In the early 1900s mining in the city limits nearly ceased and spread to an area seventy-five miles east and west and fifty miles north and south. Joplin, however, had developed every service industry necessary to mining, many of them superlative in their field, and as a result it exported products around the world. I have a very vivid recollection of negotiating a glacier in 1947 near Castrovirreyna, Peru, in the Andes at an altitude of 16,500 feet, and seeing an old crusher above me on the huge flywheel of which I clearly read, "Rogers, Joplin."

The shift of mining out of the city allowed Joplin to reform its

municipal area into a comfortable and good-looking town while retaining almost all the management and service for the greatly enlarged mining district.

The mining collapsed. It went downhill from 1949 and ceased completely in 1976. This was a disastrous blow to Joplin, one from which many cities in the West never recovered. But Joplin had been built and sustained by rugged individualism. Its citizens used these qualities to meet the challenge to its life caused by the mining collapse and successfully developed sufficient cooperation so that the city was sustained.

Joplin and its immediate area improved in every way, and increased its population and products. The mining services turned into ones that benefited new industries and agriculture. Several of its services—medical, transportation, and education—became outstanding.

Many feel as I do. This is a very pleasant place to live—the climate is seasonal, there is ample rain and sun, beautiful trees, and lush, clear creeks. In both its physical and its allegorical meaning, I remember the wisdom of Solomon who said (Song of Songs, 2:11,12):

For lo the winter is past,
The rain is over and gone;
The flowers appear on the earth;
The time of the singing of birds is come,
And the voice of the dove is heard in the land.
Philip L. Jones

Grand Falls, in southwest Joplin, contains a dam which impounds a mile-long lake that serves as a reservoir for the city's water supply. Photo by G.K. Renner

CHAPTER ONE

A Long, Thin Line of Settlement

Joplin Creek today bears little resemblance to the stream that existed at this point where Moffet and Sergeant sank their Discovery Shaft in August 1870 and touched off the boom that led to the founding of Joplin. The location is in Landreth Park, approximately 500 feet north of the new Vernon Sigars viaduct. Photo by G.K. Renner

One day in the late 1820s a strange figure appeared in Jackson County, Tennessee. Clad in buckskin and speaking broken English, young people thought he was an apparition but older residents recognized him as Edmund Jennings who, as a restless youth, had left some fifteen years earlier seeking adventure in the distant West. He told of hunting, trapping, fishing, and living with the Indians in the "Country of the Six Boils." Because of Jennings' corrupt speech, his friends misinterpreted the term as the "Country of the Six Bulls," and this version became popularized. Actually, he was referring to what is now southwest Missouri, southeast Kansas, and northeast Oklahoma where the streams of North Fork, Center Creek, Turkey Creek, Shoal Creek, Indian Creek, and Elk River converge into Spring River. These spring-fed, swiftly flowing streams had a boiling, surging quality that gave rise to the term "boils." Here, situated between Turkey and Shoal creeks and centered on Joplin Creek, the city of Joplin would grow. Many neighbors were enthralled with Jennings' tales of adventure and some decided to go to this virgin land.

The area had much to offer. Located at the western edge of the Ozark plateau where the highlands blend with the Osage Plain to the north and with the Great Plains to the west, the region featured sizeable streams close to one another. Fed largely by springs from the rocky Ozark highlands, these streams were remarkably clear and pure. Along them were broad strips of rich bottom land covered with a dense growth of oak, black walnut, and other hardwoods. Beyond the wooded areas along the streams and the hills stretched expanses of prairie, rank in the late summer with wild grass that sometimes stood as high as a man's head.

The region abounded in wild game. Along the edges of the timber herds of deer and elk grazed. Flocks of wild turkeys were common and black bears roamed the woods. On the prairies an occasional herd of buffalo could be seen. Streams were filled with fish and along the banks beaver and muskrat tempted the trapper.

This combination of resources made the Country of the Six Boils attractive to hunters and farmers. The natural springs offered ideal homesites and the timber provided a plentiful supply of wood for building and fencing. Corn could be grown in the rich bottom soil and the prairies provided a natural pasture for livestock. The relatively mild winters allowed livestock to remain outdoors with minimum care. Beneath the soil lay riches of minerals that were only dimly perceived by the early pioneers.

Prior to the arrival of white settlers, the Osage Indians, a strong and warlike tribe, dominated the central and western Ozarks for hundreds of years. Regarding the Country of the Six Boils as one of their favorite hunting grounds, the Osage hunted until December of each year when they retired to their winter lodges along the Osage River.

After the United States acquired this area as part of the Louisiana Purchase in 1803, treaties were negotiated in which the Osage agreed to withdraw completely from the new state of Missouri. However, it was not until 1831 that a trickle of settlers began to move into this country, and even then most of them stayed out of the western part where Osage hunting parties occasionally plundered the homesteads of new settlers.

A turning point came in 1837 when the Osage experienced a bad crop year. Seized with a longing for their old hunting grounds, the Osage crossed the border into the Spring River area. Governor Lilburn W. Boggs sent the state militia to the Sarcoxie area on two different occasions but no violence resulted because the Indians either fled or surrendered and were escorted out of the state. Recorded in state documents as the Osage War and known popularly as the Sarcoxie War, this disturbance marked the end of the Indian threat in southwest Missouri after which the tempo of settlement increased markedly.

Once ownership passed to the United States, Americans began moving into what became the state of Missouri and settlement formed a distinct "T" pattern as pioneers spread up the valleys of the Mississippi and Missouri rivers where water transportation was readily available. The Ozarks enjoyed no such natural advantages. No river cut through the rugged hills of the eastern Ozarks to empty directly into the Mississippi River. To the west, the Osage River flowed along the northwestern edge of the Ozark plateau, emptying into the Missouri River in the central part of the state. To the southeast, the White River cut through the northern Arkansas Ozarks with a segment looping into southern Missouri before veering southeast to empty into the Arkansas River at its confluence with the Mississippi. On the western side, the Spring River flowed through the Country of the Six Boils before emptying into the Grand River which ran south to the Arkansas River. None of these routes offered fully navigable waters and all involved journeying around the periphery of the Ozarks for hundreds of miles.

A long, thin stream of pioneers, first hunters and then farmers, began moving up the White River into what became southwest Missouri. Edmund Jennings and other solitary hunters evidently operated in the region and had connections for marketing their furs and hides.

A contemporary of Jennings, the naturalist Henry Rowe Schoolcraft, visited southwest Missouri and northwest Arkansas in 1818 and vividly described the life of the early hunters and trappers. Traveling on the upper reaches of the White River, Schoolcraft encountered a string of cabins. The settlers downriver hunted and raised corn, but the inhabitants of the isolated cabins farther upstream were semi-nomadic hunters. They floated rafts loaded with skins, honey, bear bacon, and buffalo meat to trading points downstream where they bartered these products for necessary goods. Schoolcraft reported that the men were skilled hunters but "slaves to their dogs," the only thing around them to which they appeared truly devoted. Staying with one of these families for a few days, he reported they subsisted on a steady diet of hominy and bear meat with sassafras tea for breakfast.

Permanent settlers did not arrive in the Country of the Six Boils until the 1830s. Thacker Vivion became the first settler in what is now eastern Jasper County. Vivion, an emigrant from Kentucky, settled at the site of Sarcoxie in 1831. Within a few months he built a gristmill and a sawmill. Fourteen more families arrived in 1833 and the following year, when William Tingle and Ben F. Massey opened a general store, the little settlement began to take on the appearance of a village.

Settlement in the western part of the county came more slowly. Evidently the first settler in what is now Joplin was John C. Cox. A Tennessean, Cox was fascinated by Edmund Jennings' tales of adventure and at the urging of Nathan Boone, son of the famous explorer, Cox came to the Joplin area in 1836 on a scouting mission. Pleased with the new area, he left Tennessee in early 1838 accompanied by his young bride and his sister. Arriving on Turkey Creek, Cox built a log cabin and lived there until 1841 when he moved to a more substantial log house at 615 Persimmon Street and built a store nearby. Cox named the store and accompanying post office, Blytheville, in honor of his friend, Billy Blythe, a Cherokee Indian who lived on Shoal Creek. Though the store thrived, a settlement did not develop at the Blytheville location.

The year 1839 marked the arrival of the Reverend Harris G. Joplin. According to census records, Joplin was born in 1807 in North Carolina but grew up in Tennessee. He had four children by his first wife, Holly Sims, and two by his second wife, Mary Whipple. Joplin, a Methodist minister, built a cabin at a spring

Top: John C. Cox, often called the father of Joplin, moved to the area in 1838 and operated the store and post office in Blytheville for thirty years. He was a respected community leader and served as a county judge and a justice of the peace. Courtesy, Dorothea B. Hoover Historical Museum

Bottom: This is a rare portrait of Mrs. John C. Cox. Born Sarah Ann Mercer in 1816, she and her husband moved to Missouri in 1838, arriving on Turkey Creek just thirteen days before the birth of their first child, Lucy Jane. Courtesy, Dorothea B. Hoover Historical Museum

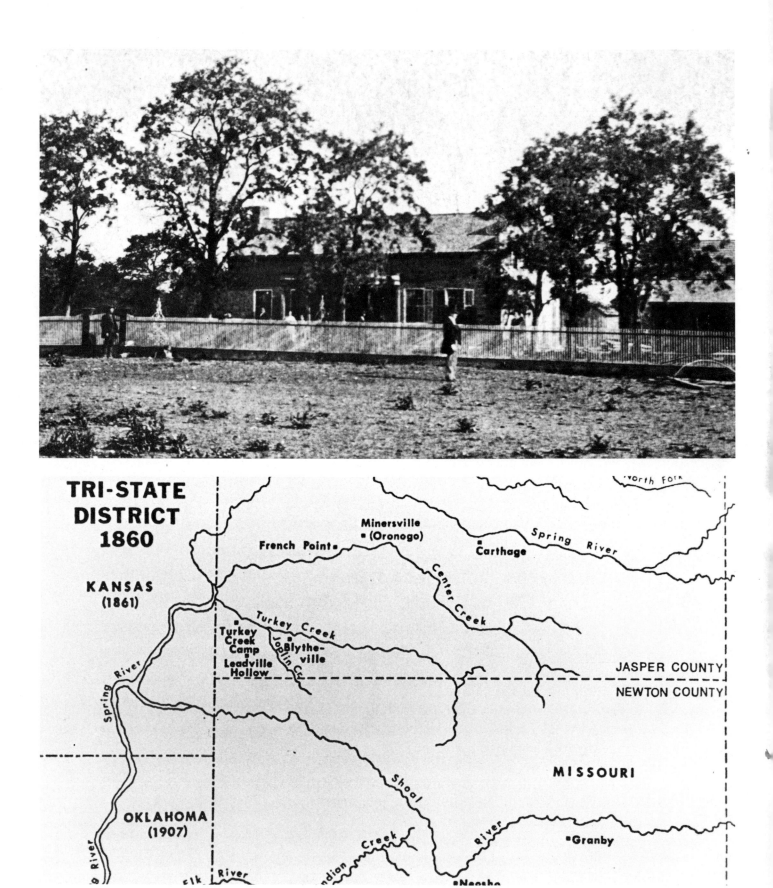

Facing page, top: This was John C. Cox's home shortly after its completion in 1866. It was located just east of his earlier home and store that were destroyed during the Civil War. Known as Wig Hill, the house is owned by descendants of Cox. Courtesy, Dorothea B. Hoover Historical Museum

Bottom: The streams that gave rise to the name, "Country of the Six Boils" are evident in this map that also shows the chief mining camps of 1860. Except for Spring River, these streams were not generally navigable during the rainy season. At that time, rafts loaded with agricultural products or lead might be floated downstream. The long-term trend, as roads improved, was to haul the goods by wagon to points where they could be loaded directly onto steamboats. From Wilderness Bonanza, by Arrell M. Gibson, 1972

Right: William Tingle, shown here in a rare photograph, was one of Jasper County's earliest pioneers. With his business partners, Tingle developed Leadville, one of the leading mining camps of the antebellum era. After the Civil War, Tingle lived near Turkey Creek until he died in 1904. He is buried in Peace Church Cemetery. Courtesy, Dorothea B. Hoover Historical Museum

near the Blytheville post office (near the intersection of Fifth and Club streets) where he held services and organized the first Methodist congregation in western Jasper County. An eloquent speaker, Joplin's slender build, fair complexion, clean-shaven face, and close-cropped hair presented a striking figure. The spring on which he settled formed a branch that ran westward about one-half mile to a creek. In time, Joplin's name became attached to the spring and the creek. Financial reverses in operating his eighty-acre farm forced Joplin to leave the area in late 1844. The following year he helped locate and plat the town of Mount Vernon, and shortly afterward, Joplin moved to Springfield where he lived until his death in about 1853.

Though early Jasper Countians did not live in the mainstream of a money economy, life could be satisfying. Pioneers built log cabins along streams, often at one of the many natural springs. Corn and hay were the principal agricultural crops although some cotton was grown for cloth and sheep were raised for wool. Cattle grazed on the abundant grass in the prairies and hogs were often fattened on acorns in the woods. Plowing and other heavy work was usually done with oxen. Wild game, particularly deer and turkey, were plentiful but so were wolves, and lambs and pigs had to be protected from these and other predators.

With the Mexican War between 1846 and 1848 and the California Gold Rush in 1849, Jasper Countians found a growing market for their livestock. Cattle and herds of horses and mules were driven north to Westport, Independence, and other Missouri points where wagon trains formed for the long westward trek. Also, the extension of the cotton belt into the Mississippi valley opened up new southern markets, particularly for mules. But the high cost of transportation limited the markets open to farmers. Only those products that possessed a high value in relation to their weight and bulk, or that could be driven on the hoof, could be marketed profitably.

Another source of income lay in the deposits of lead and zinc underlying portions of the area, but an awareness of their potential came slowly. Small deposits of ore had been discovered as early as 1836, but serious development of the ore bodies did not begin until 1849 when David Campbell, an experienced miner from eastern Missouri, found lead ore on a farm owned by William Tingle about two miles northwest of the present city of Joplin. The area, popularly known as "Shakerag," soon blossomed into a small mining camp named Leadville.

At the same time Thomas Livingston, Judge Andrew McKee, and their partners developed a discovery of lead on Center Creek near the site of earlier diggings. A town known as Minersville (later Oronogo) soon developed and a smelter was installed at nearby French Point. Some 419,000 pounds of refined lead had been produced there by 1855 and by 1860 Minersville was a thriving mining camp.

In the same time period, Judge Cox's slave boy, Pete, digging for fishing worms on the banks of Joplin Creek near the Blytheville post office, unearthed chunks of lead ore. Though little mining took place at this time, the discovery later led to the founding of Joplin.

The arrival of Campbell and other experienced miners marked a turning point. Up to this time the unearthing of isolated deposits of lead was of no great significance because similar findings had been made in every county in southern Missouri. The arrival of professional miners, however, signified a growing awareness that the deposits were extensive enough to support full-scale mining.

Discoveries of even greater immediate importance were made at this time on Shoal Creek in Newton County, the most significant of which was at Granby in 1850. Farther down Shoal Creek, between Granby and Neosho, J.W. Moseley also developed an extensive operation.

The Jasper and Newton county mining operations might well have developed into a boom had it not been for the formidable transportation problems. Though some lead was rafted down Spring River, most of the output of the Jasper County mines probably went by wagon to Osceola on the Osage River or to Booneville where it was loaded onto Missouri River steamers. These arrangements were expensive. Contemporary observers realized that lead production in southwest Missouri, feasible only when prices were high, would remain limited until railroads were built.

Jasper County grew substantially during the 1850s. The census of 1860 showed a population of 6,883, an increase of approximately 60 percent over 1850. Nevertheless, large expanses of the county were virtually empty and the largest towns were mere villages. In the 1860 census no separate count was made, but the estimated population of the four largest municipalities was: Carthage-500, Sarcoxie-400, Sherwood-250, and Minersville-100. Without railroads the area remained remote and thirty years of settlement had brought only a thin stream of immigrants. People looked expectantly to the railroads to end their isolation. The southwest branch of the Pacific Railroad had been built to Rolla, some 200 miles away, but a decade would pass before trains arrived in Jasper County and in the intervening years the area would be devastated by civil war.

This road scene, in which the lady's loyalty is being challenged, was common during the Civil War. Many people attempted to remain neutral but mounting violence forced them to take sides. Early in the war Confederate guerrilla bands forced many Unionists to flee, but later, as Union army troops gained firmer control, the Secessionists felt compelled to leave. From Sketchbook, by Robert O. Sweeney. Courtesy, State Historical Society of Missouri

Though a part of the slaveholding South, Jasper County's 335 slaves in 1860 accounted for only about 5 percent of the population. Most families were nonslaveholders. It is not clear if a majority of the people supported slavery, but as Wiley Britton points out in his book, *Pioneer Life in Southwest Missouri,* the "real public opinion molders, the preachers and the politicians," supported the institution and generated sympathy for the Southern cause. Most Jasper Countians were initially perplexed by the threat to the Union, but increased hostilities polarized them between the Secessionists and the Unionists.

Secessionist sentiment was strongest in Sarcoxie. As early as 1858 a mob tarred and feathered a schoolteacher of abolitionist leaning who had read *Uncle Tom's Cabin* to his pupils. Sarcoxie also flew the first Confederate flag in the state. The emblem was twenty-seven feet long and flew from a pole nearly 100 feet high until it was cut down by Union troops.

Jasper County became an early battleground in the war because it was located adjacent to the free territory of Kansas (where border clashes over slavery had been occurring since 1854) and because the region provided a natural gateway to the South along the western edge of the Ozark Mountains. The region's lead mines also were of strategic importance. In the fall of 1861 the Granby mines were supplying much of the South's lead but the next year Northern troops regained control of the mines. After this, lead shipments dwindled as intensifying guerrilla activity left mining camps abandoned.

The first important battle occurred at Carthage on July 5, 1861, when the Union force of Colonel Franz Sigel, consisting largely of German troops from St. Louis, clashed with the Missouri State Guard commanded by Governor Claiborne F. Jackson. Sigel's force of 1,100 men, outnumbered by five to one, was forced to fall back through Carthage and eventually withdraw to Springfield. This clash, one of the earliest battles of the Civil War, left the Secessionists in control of Jasper County and magnified pro-Southern sympathy.

Wiley Britton has left us a vivid personal account of the pro-Southern guerrilla activity that swept the region in the wake of the Battle of Carthage. Worried about his family, who were outspoken Unionists, Britton journeyed from Fort Scott, Kansas, to the family home on Shoal Creek between Neosho and Grand Falls. Arriving in Grand Falls, friends directed him to where his father and brother were hiding in the woods to avoid being seized by the Secessionists. That night Britton visited his mother and younger brothers and sisters at home, talking to them in the dark because of the danger of lighting a lamp. Britton led his father and brother safely back to Kansas while his mother and the children stayed on the farm, only to lose most of their live-stock, grain, and hay to guerrillas.

Men were in the most danger from the guerrillas, or bushwack-ers, as they were called. These marauding bands would kill the men but leave women and children unmolested. It was not un-common—as with the Britton family—to find women struggling to operate the farm and care for the children while the men were in hiding or had fled the county. Stories of women and children cutting the bodies of loved ones down from trees where they had been hung and rolling them into shallow graves were common.

While the Confederate government tried to maintain con-trol over the guerrilla bands, many operated with little restraint. Union guerrilla groups often operated out of Kansas and were called Jayhawkers. In Missouri, Union garrisons were main-tained at Carthage, Cave Springs, Mount Vernon, Newtonia, and Neosho.

Unionists remained under heavy pressure until the third year of the war. Judge Cox fled to Neosho and his home and store at Blytheville were burned. In May 1862 a train of thirty to forty wagons left Jasper County for Fort Scott. Escorted by federal troops, the wagons were piled high with the household goods of Unionist refugees while herds of livestock trailed along behind. Later in the war, when Union troops gained control, Secessionists felt endangered and many of them also fled.

The most effective of the local Confederate guerrilla chief-tains was Thomas R. Livingston. A French Point lead miner, Livingston had been something of a brawler in the rough saloons of the mining camps before the war. His cavalrymen dressed in ordinary civilian clothes, and armed with carbines and three or four Colt revolvers thrust in their belts, were a formidable foe in the numerous skirmishes in the district. Livingston died in an attack at Stockton, Missouri, in July 1863.

Sherwood, now part of Carl Junction, was the leading commer-cial center of western Jasper County and became the focal point of many area skirmishes. It was burned by federal troops in 1863 after a clash between the First Kansas Colored Infantry Regiment, which operated briefly in the area, and Livingston's guerrillas. Completely devastated, as was the countryside surrounding it, Sherwood was never rebuilt.

In the late summer of 1864, fighting intensified as General Sterling Price's Confederate army of 12,000 entered Missouri and touched off a flurry of guerrilla activity. In the resulting confu-sion, Carthage was left temporarily unguarded and guerrillas burned virtually the entire town. With the courthouse already destroyed, the Jasper County government moved to Cave Springs and remained there until after the war.

The last six months of the Civil War were relatively quiet in Jasper County, but the coming of peace in the spring of 1865 left a sorely ravaged county. Sarcoxie was partially destroyed. Livestock roamed freely in the countryside because the fences had been burned. Herds of deer, flocks of wild turkeys and other animals had increased tremendously during the war. Wolves were so tame that they could be shot from wagons that moved along the seldom-used roads.

But hope was not a casualty of the war. Though many pro-Southern families never returned, Union soldiers, who had served here during the war and liked the area, came back to live. The large expanses of abandoned land offered the opportunities of an open frontier but a basic structure of roads, communities, and local governments had survived and provided a foundation on which the area could quickly rebuild.

William Clarke Quantrill was a notorious Confederate guerrilla chieftain. This drawing of Quantrill and his men, titled "The Council," might well have been near Joplin. In October 1863 Quantrill attacked Union army General James G. Blunt's wagon train near Baxter Springs; eighty Union soldiers died in the ensuing battle while Quantrill lost only one man. From Outlaws of the Border. *Courtesy, State Historical Society of Missouri*

A Mining Boomtown

Settlers began to pour into Jasper County after 1865. Though the wartime devastation had forced most of the population to flee, by 1870 the county had 14,928 people, more than double the census figure of ten years before. The area had much to offer the prospective immigrant. In 1865 Jasper County had over 100,000 acres of public lands available, much of it forfeited by refugees who never returned. Fine prairie land sold for as little as two dollars per acre.

Another stimulant to resettlement was the resumption of lead mining. In 1867 the Granby Mining and Smelting Company began acquiring large tracts of land and under the stimulus of this company Minersville grew to 350 residents by 1869. In that year the growing town changed its name to Oronogo.

The Granby company stimulated development by leasing small tracts to miners, and in doing so, set the stage for the founding of Joplin. In the spring of 1870 the company offered a reward of $500 to the leaseholder who mined the most lead in a stipulated period of time. The prize went to two Oronogo miners, Elliott R. Moffet and John B. Sergeant.

Encouraged to strike out on their own by this $500 grubstake, Moffet and Sergeant scouted the old diggings along Joplin Creek for a likely prospect. In August 1870 they leased a ten-acre tract from John Cox and began sinking a shaft on the east bank of the creek. The exact location of their "Discovery Shaft" is unknown, but it was approximately 500 feet north of the old Broadway viaduct. The oft-repeated story is that the partners, struggling in the late summer heat, had exhausted their supplies and in an act of near desperation, borrowed blasting powder for their final shot. Luckily it uncovered a rich body of ore at about the thirty-five or forty foot level. The shaft reportedly produced $60,000 worth of lead in the first ninety days.

The Moffet and Sergeant discovery sparked a sustained boom that led to the founding of Joplin and eventually made it the leading city of the Tri-State mining district. A year after the initial discovery some 500 people had settled in the small valley, living in tents, pole shelters covered with brush, and makeshift box houses.

As the Joplin Creek mining camp mushroomed in population,

Top: Elliott R. Moffet moved to Oronogo in 1867 and became Joplin's first mayor in 1873. This portrait was made circa 1873. Courtesy, Tri-State Mineral Museum

Bottom: John B. Sergeant was the senior member of the legendary partnership of Moffet and Sergeant whose Discovery Shaft in the Joplin Creek valley led to the founding of Joplin. Retiring from mining in 1880, Sergeant invested his money in several Joplin businesses, most notably the first railroad and the first streetcar line. Courtesy, Tri-State Mineral Museum

John Cox saw the need for town lots and on July 28, 1871, he filed a plat for a new municipality named Joplin City centered at about Broadway and Cox. This original townsite encompassed seventeen acres, and though Cox later platted an additional twenty-three acres, he was reluctant to play the role of entrepreneur and sold much of his land to other developers.

Across the creek valley, plans were underway to found another new town. Patrick Murphy, a Carthage merchant, his partner William P. Davis, and other associates purchased a forty-acre tract from Oliver Picher and filed a plat for a new town on September 4, 1871, centered at about Fourth and Main. It was named Murphysburg after its principal founder.

The two new towns grew rapidly. Murphy and Davis built a miners supply store at First and Main streets, and shortly afterward, a smelter. Lots were sold on liberal terms. If a purchaser would buy one and build a house on it, Murphy would give him another lot. Main Street was widened from sixty feet to eighty feet and numerous businesses sprang up to cater to the needs of the mushrooming population. As 1872 drew to a close, approximately 2,000 people lived in the two towns, an increase of more than 1,500 in less than six months.

In the fall of 1871 John H. Taylor, an Independence attorney who became a leader in Joplin's development, organized the Joplin Mining and Smelting Company. Taylor and his Kansas City associates purchased 120 acres of John Cox's land located north of Fourth Street. Their control of a segment of the Joplin Creek valley where Union Station would later be built led to this area being called the Kansas City Bottoms.

With the growth of the Joplin mining camp, lawlessness became a severe problem. Saloon and street fights were common as was indiscriminate shooting, particularly at windows. Though there were few robberies or murders, the rowdyism reached such intensity that the period became known as the Reign of Terror.

Since Joplin City and Murphysburg legally existed only as plats filed with the county recorder, the only local government came through the organization of Galena and Joplin townships. Clearly a municipal government was needed and in February 1872 a number of citizens met at Brazelle's store in Murphysburg to consider incorporating the settlements. During the deliberations Patrick Murphy argued that the only way to deal effectively with the law-and-order problem was to unite the two settlements. Accordingly, a petition was presented to the Jasper County Court and that body ordered the two towns incorporated under the name of Union City on March 14, 1872. The new municipal authorities then appointed a marshal and built a jail on Broadway, the main thoroughfare linking the two towns. The new marshal, J.W. Lipton, soon became something of a hero when he subdued "Dutch Pete," the notorious bully of Murphysburg. After this the Reign of Terror came to an end.

Union brought stability and a degree of permanency as men began bringing their families to the new town. Mining also continued to expand as three new camps—Lone Elm, Parr Hill, and Swindle Hill—opened in 1872.

While union stabilized the law-and-order problem, it did not dissolve the deep-seated jealousy that had developed between the two settlements. While both towns were about equal in population, Murphysburg had developed the largest business district and was outpacing Joplin City in growth. Joplin City residents in particular felt discriminated against in police protection and taxation. The crowning grievance came when the Blytheville post office was closed in favor of a new Union City establishment on the west side. A Joplin City saloon operator initiated a lawsuit to dissolve the incorporation of Union City on the grounds that the original petition contained invalid signatures. In December 1872 a judicial court upheld the challenge and voided the incorporation. The Jasper County Court then moved to reinstate the separate towns of Joplin City and Murphysburg.

The two towns might have remained separate municipalities had not a group of dynamic leaders envisioned a future for their town as a leading metropolitan center if the rival factions could be brought together. Soon an election was held in which the people voted in favor of another merger, but this time civic leaders applied to the state legislature for a special charter giving the new town status as a fourth-class city. Patrick Murphy gave strong impetus to the new union when he accepted the name Joplin, thus submerging his own namesake of Murphysburg. The state legislature approved the charter bill on March 23, 1873, the date that is generally accepted as the birth of the city of Joplin. The governor appointed E.R. Moffet to serve as mayor until October 14, 1873, the date of the first yearly scheduled election.

Joplin enjoyed a spectacular boom until the late 1870s. In 1875 the fledgling city already had fifty-two mercantile establishments. Additional businesses included twelve blacksmith shops, five hotels, three newspapers, two banks, and sixteen physicians. An 1882 count showed seventeen saloons in the town. Despite loose claims about the excessive number of drinking establishments in early Joplin, city fathers kept the number moderate by requiring that the application for a license be accompanied by a petition bearing the signatures of two-thirds of those who would be neighbors of the proposed saloon. Later a stiff licensing tax accom-

Murphysburg founder Patrick Murphy served as Joplin's mayor in 1875. Known for his generosity, Murphy once dropped two ten-dollar bills down a shaft where two miners, who were broke and about to abandon their lease, were digging. The money allowed them to continue and shortly afterward they made a rich strike. Courtesy, Dorothea B. Hoover Historical Museum

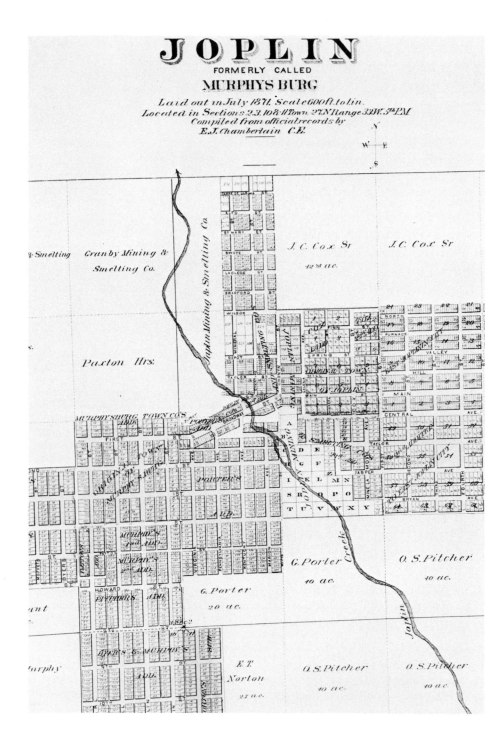

Left: This 1876 map of Joplin depicts the original plats of Joplin City and Murphysburg. Indicative of the town's rapid growth were the numerous additions that had already been made in the city's short five-year history. From Illustrated Historical Atlas of Jasper County

Facing page, top: This circa 1873 photograph is a rare view of the early Joplin mining camp. Notice that all the businesses are located in tents—an indication of the boomtown nature of the settlement. Marion Staples, the woman standing near the auctioneer's tent, was a Joplin realtor for many years. Courtesy, Rolla Stephens

Bottom: The "armstrong" windlass, one of the most primitive devices used in early-day mines, consisted of a hand-cranked wooden cylinder with a rope for hoisting the ore bucket out of the depths of a mine. Courtesy, Dorothea B. Hoover Historical Museum

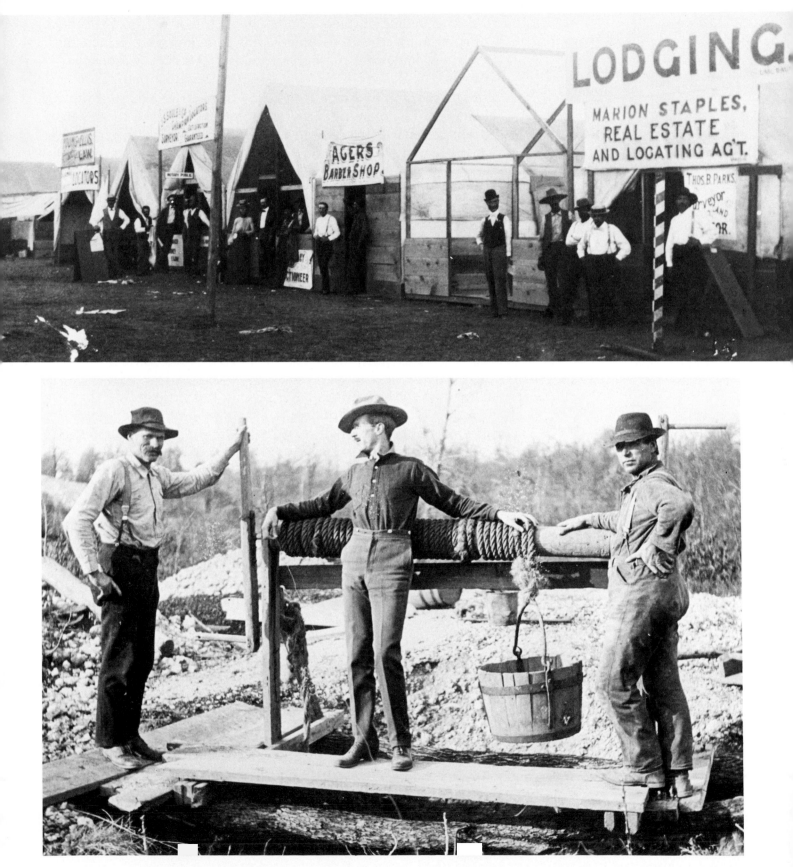

plished the same purpose.

Beginning in late 1877 Joplin's growth rate slowed, principally because of important ore discoveries at Webb City, Carterville, and Galena, Kansas. These new diggings caused an exodus of miners from Joplin where the shallow pockets of lead were nearly exhausted. The opening of the nearby camps proved to be beneficial, however, because they stimulated Joplin's growth as a wholesale and trading center for the district. The census of 1880 showed a population of 7,038. By this time the budding city was almost as large as Springfield and far larger than any of the other emerging mining towns.

A key to Joplin's continued growth lay in adequate transportation. Unfortunately the new municipality developed too late to share in the initial railroad lines that were built into the district. Even after Joplin grew into a mining center of some significance, railroad promoters regarded it as a transitory phenomenon and built toward the older, well-established towns.

By 1870 the Atlantic and Pacific Railroad, extending southwest from St. Louis, had a line running through Springfield, Pierce City, Neosho, and on into Indian Territory. In 1872 a branch railroad was completed from Pierce City to Carthage and the next year it reached Oronogo, just seven miles from Joplin. In 1870 the Kansas City, Fort Scott, and Gulf Railroad entered Baxter Springs.

By 1875 an extensive wagon freighting and stagecoach business had built up between these railheads and Joplin. Most heavy freight came by rail to Baxter Springs and then was laboriously teamed to Joplin, a route that involved fording both Spring River and Shoal Creek.

Faced with this transportation crisis, Moffet and Sergeant joined with other local investors to build a rail line that would connect with a railway at Girard, Kansas, and provide an economical way to transport fuel for the local smelters. The railroad was completed in August 1877 with a ceremony in which a symbolic lead spike was driven near the depot on Smelter Hill. Later the line merged with the St. Louis and San Francisco (Frisco) Railroad.

By the late 1870s railroad companies began to realize they could not afford to stay out of Joplin. Many of the railroads were merged into the Frisco system by the 1880s. Other railroads that entered Joplin were the Missouri Pacific, the Missouri, Kansas and Texas, and the Kansas City Southern. Mathias Splitlog, a wealthy McDonald County Indian, played a key role in bringing the latter into Joplin. The Missouri and Northern Arkansas, projected to run from Joplin to Helena, Arkansas, served Joplin but used the Kansas City Southern tracks north from Neosho.

Left: This buffalo was tied to a post in front of a butcher shop on Main Street circa 1880. Though small herds of buffalo once roamed the prairies near Joplin, they were rare by this time. Whether these solemn spectators are looking on out of curiosity or in anticipation of a buffalo steak is unclear. Courtesy, Dorothea B. Hoover Historical Museum

Below: This stagecoach, photographed in front of the Campbell Brothers Livery Stable, was probably bound for Baxter Springs. Prior to 1877, when Joplin acquired a railroad, stagecoaches or hack services were the only public carriers available to travelers. The hack fare to Carthage was twenty-five cents. Courtesy, Dorothea B. Hoover Historical Museum

A major problem of any growing city is the provision of municipal services. As Joplin made the transition from a mining camp to a town, one of the most pressing needs was a municipal water system. Heavy mining soon polluted the natural water supply and the public came to depend on water haulers who brought in fresh water from outlying areas and filled the water barrels of homeowners and businesses. Many homeowners also kept rain barrels which were a good source of water for laundering.

Business leaders felt that the lack of adequate water was hindering the development of manufacturing in Joplin. In a special election, citizens voted heavily in favor of a water system and the Joplin Water Works Company was organized. The planners showed great foresight by bringing in water from Shoal Creek, four miles beyond the city limits. By turning to this plentiful supply of spring-fed water, the engineers created a basic system that has served Joplin for more than 100 years. The water first flowed through the thirteen miles of mains on November 1, 1881.

Many other services were added during these years of transition. In 1877, four years before the waterworks was completed, the Joplin Gas and Coke Company began providing gas (manufactured out of coal) for street lighting and for houses. Telephones were first installed in Joplin in 1881. The next year John B. Sergeant organized the Joplin Street Railway Company to provide public transportation. The original line ran from East Joplin to Smelter Hill. The cars, called "dinkies," ran on iron-strapped wooden rails and were pulled by mules. Joplin citizens were first dazzled by electric lights when the Cole Circus performed in 1882. Five years later, G.W. Sergeant, son of city father John B., built a generating plant on Joplin Street and set up an exhibition light at Fourth and Main. He soon won a street lighting contract for the downtown district. The crude carbon-arc lights hissed and sputtered, but they were a harbinger of a new era.

Joplin, or rather Union City, first organized a volunteer fire department in 1872. This system, called the Bucket Brigade, required that every businessman keep a water barrel and a bucket in front of his establishment and respond in case of a fire. Not surprisingly, a whole business block in East Joplin was wiped out by fire late that year. After this the city bought fire engines and organized the volunteers into companies. In 1882, after completion of the water system with its sixty-five fire hydrants, the department was completely reorganized but remained volunteer. Firemen drew $1.50 for each call and the first company to throw water on a fire received a $10 prize. In 1893 a paid fire department was established.

The growth of mining soon spawned many support institutions. Joplin's first bank, the National Savings Bank, opened in 1872 at Galena and Broadway in East Joplin, but soon closed. Patrick Murphy organized the Miners' Bank in 1882 and Thomas W. Cunningham incorporated the Bank of Joplin, which is remembered as one of the few institutions at the turn of the century to employ women.

Churches were established very quickly in the new town. Methodists initially held services in Bullock and Boucher's saloon with the minister preaching from behind the bar until a structure was built at Fourth and Kentucky. In the fall of 1872 the Southern Methodists established a church and shared a building with the Presbyterians until 1876. African Methodists also organized in 1872 and met in homes until 1881 when they purchased the old Methodist church building. Catholics, Baptists, Christians, and Episcopalians also established churches during this time. In 1876 the Congregationalists organized the Tabernacle Church which was used for public meetings.

The first two decades of Joplin's existence marked the evolution of a unified school system for the new town. With urban growth, the old Franklin school district, which once served most of southwest Jasper County, became the East Joplin school district and in 1873 this district completed the Washington School. West Joplin formed a separate school district over the opposition of the east-side residents, as did Lone Elm. Short of funds, the West Joplin district operated for several years out of rented buildings and the "Old Brick School" at Fourth and Pennsylvania.

A separate school for blacks, as required by law, was maintained jointly by the east and west Joplin districts because of low enrollment. A count in 1882 showed only seventy-nine black children of school age.

No formal high school program was offered before 1886. In that year the West Joplin district organized a three-year high school curriculum at the Central School. The first class, consisting of thirteen members, graduated in 1888.

During the 1880s a movement to unite the school districts grew as rivalries and jealousies between East and West Joplin subsided. In 1889 voters approved consolidation.

A few private schools were set up in Joplin. The most important of these was Our Lady of Mercy Convent established by the Sisters of Mercy in 1885. Also, Dr. J.C. Petit established the Joplin College of Physicians and Surgeons that operated briefly in East Joplin.

A growing town needs a newspaper and publishers quickly filled this need. In 1872 Peter Schnur established *Mining News,*

Joplin's first newspaper. Three years later it became the *Joplin Daily News,* the town's first daily. In 1877 A.W. Carson established the weekly *Sunday Herald* which, a few months later, became the *Daily Herald.* Democratic in tone, the *Herald* merged with the Republican *Daily News* in 1900 to form the *News Herald.* The *Joplin Daily Globe,* founded in 1896, was purchased by A.H. Rogers in 1910, and under the leadership of the Rogers family, the *Globe* absorbed the *News Herald* in 1922 and became Joplin's only major publisher.

Early-day Joplin was a hard-working boomtown but the people also yearned for entertainment and soon a rich variety of amusements were available. The Joplin Opera House, Blackwell's Opera House, and the Haven Opera House appeared downtown in the mid-1870s. At this time it was not uncommon for miners to wheel a barrow full of lead to a theater to pay for tickets.

In 1879 Patrick Murphy organized Joplin Exposition amusement park which occupied a forty-acre tract in southwest Joplin and featured a racetrack as well as exhibition facilities. Annual fairs were held in this amusement center, later known as Barbee Park.

Lonely miners, who had left their families behind, often found entertainment in the local saloons. Many featured full orchestras and were open on Sunday, as were most businesses. In 1876 some 1,200 spectators watched a fight, sponsored by Blackwell's saloon, between a cinnamon bear and six bulldogs. The bear won.

Fourth of July celebrations always prompted a large turnout of people. The 1876 celebration was held at the newly opened Schifferdecker Gardens located on Turkey Creek near Castle Rock. This amusement center provided a dance pavilion and bowling lanes, and offered cool beer from Schifferdecker's cave. The 1885 celebration at Castle Rock park featured the usual parade, band concert, and fireworks plus a mock Revolutionary War battle.

Circuses played frequently and were always popular. In the 1880s the Mardi Gras celebrations were a key attraction. Joplin's many lodges, like the Masons, Elks, and Odd Fellows, featured social activities. Roller skating became a recreational fad in the late 1870s. Because the skaters ordinarily used the Tabernacle Church hall for their sessions, wags called them the "Holy Rollers."

Joplin grew rapidly during the 1880s. In 1887 citizens voted in favor of becoming a third-class city. This new charter proved to be a milestone in municipal development because it opened the way for civic improvements such as street paving, the construction of sewer lines, and the strengthening of police regulations. The new municipality was evolving from a rough mining town to a city.

Facing page, top: Dr. Julius C. Petit established the Joplin College of Physicians and Surgeons, on Broadway in East Joplin, in 1880. Petit's activities were severely criticized by Joplin's medical fraternity and in 1881 three shots were fired at him through a window as he sat at his desk. Dr. Petit gave up management of the institute in 1883 and it burned a year later. From The History of Jasper County, *by F.A. North, 1883*

Bottom: The Joplin Opera House, at Second and Main, was photographed in June 1879. Located above two mercantile stores, the hall had a large stage and seated 600 people. This building burned after a performance in November 1881 and was quickly rebuilt. Courtesy, Dorothea B. Hoover Historical Museum

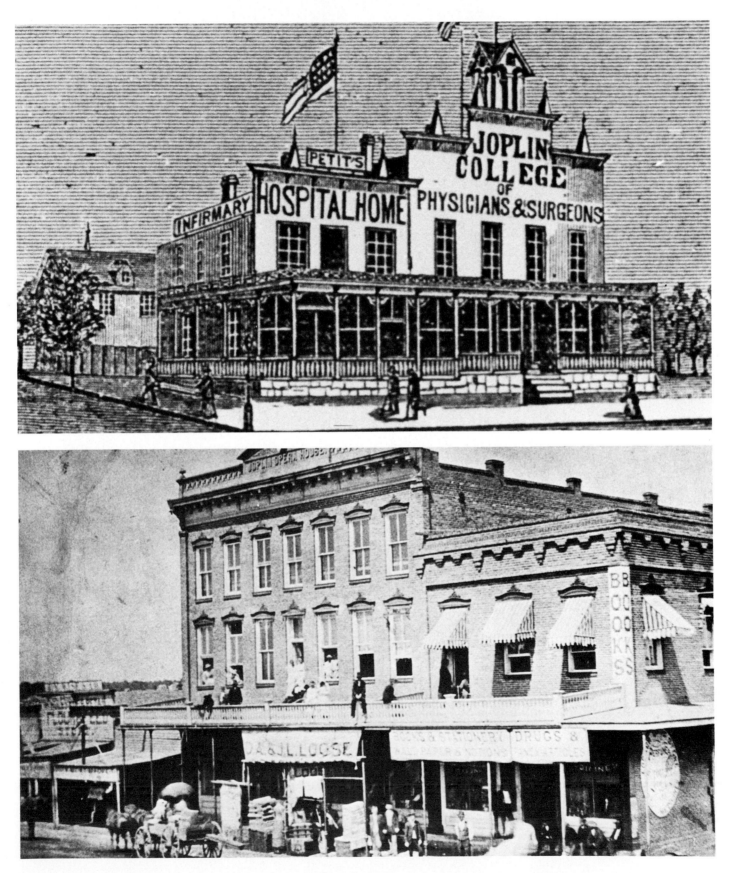

CHAPTER THREE
Capital of the Tri-State District

Joplin experienced its most rapid growth between 1890 and 1910. The census of 1890 revealed a population of 9,943 in the young city, a healthy 41 percent increase over the 1880 figure. With its emerging railroad connections, its dominance in the manufacturing of mining machinery, and its growing importance in the financing and administration of mining, Joplin was rapidly consolidating its position as the hub of the Tri-State district.

Changes came to the mining industry during this time, particularly in the area of mechanization. Power-driven rock drills and hoisting equipment became common while steam-powered churn drills took over the job of prospecting for new ore. Electrically driven machines came into use starting in 1890. While most mines had their own concentration mills where the rock was separated from the galena (lead ore) or jack (zinc ore), shoveling continued to be a hand operation and underground ore cars were either pushed by hand or pulled by mules.

The lease system of mining continued into the new century. Outside capital began to move into the area from eastern and foreign sources, but most of it was invested in land and royalty companies that bought up acreage or leases. This resulted in a process called "pyramiding of royalties" in which mine operators found themselves paying royalties to one, two, or even more leaseholders who sandwiched themselves between the operators and the landowners. As a result, royalty charges began to rise.

This pyramiding of holdings by land and royalty companies reached a peak by 1900. The Granby Mining and Smelting Company remained the largest at the turn of the century. At that time it held 20,000 acres of land, 988 of which were in Joplin. The Rex Mining and Smelting Company controlled the "Thousand Acre" tract just outside the Joplin city limits, extending eastward from Range Line to Duquesne Road and south from Thirteenth to Thirty-second streets. The Missouri Lead and Zinc Company held a total of 1,300 acres of land, its 760 acres within Joplin were from Missouri Avenue to Range Line and southward from Sixth to Thirty-second streets.

Though these land and royalty companies provided services to mining operators such as prospecting through drilling, pumping water, and supplying gas, electricity, and low-cost housing for miners, their profits meant that the natural wealth of the Tri-State district was being siphoned off by outside capitalists rather than being reinvested in local growth and development.

Unusual names and personalities seemed to be always associated with the mining industry. Operators tried to outdo one another with distinctive names for their diggings. Names such as Yellow Dog and Green Dog were in vogue at one time and others went by such names as Jack Pot, Holy Moses, and Little Hope. An impoverished preacher, driven out of Kansas by the grasshopper plague, called his mine the Grasshopper Diggings. Grubstaked by Patrick Murphy, he became wealthy when he struck a rich vein of galena. Mrs. M.C. Allen operated a mine in Blendville and she became known as Joplin's first "mining queen." Early in the century Mrs. Morgan took over the operation of a mine in southeast Joplin from her husband. Riding ore buckets down the shaft like a veteran, Mrs. Morgan made frequent inspection trips into the mine. Trying to sell the mine, she is said to have brought in a load of extra-rich ore from a neighboring operation to impress an eastern buyer. Reportedly she sold the mine, which was a good producer, for $50,000.

The mining district's work force at the turn of the century numbered about 10,000. Many miners were farmers who worked part-time to supplement their income while a number of others were prospectors, down on their luck, who intended to work only long enough to save up another grubstake. The standard workweek was fifty-four hours, consisting of six, nine-hour days until a law was passed in 1899 that reduced the work day to eight hours. Wages were about $2 per day with shovelers earning more.

Most of the migratory miners lived in boarding houses. These establishments, often run by the wives or widows of miners, usually charged seven dollars per week for breakfast, a lunch bucket, and bed. No bath was provided. The major land and royalty companies sometimes allowed miners to build on company land. In 1900 the Missouri Lead and Zinc Company laid out a camp large enough for 350 houses on their land between Missouri Avenue and the Kansas City Southern Railroad tracks. Built on lots often just twenty-five feet wide, the shacks had one or two rooms—usually a combination living and bedroom in front and a kitchen in back, with a front and back door and two windows on each side. The Missouri company charged one dollar per month ground rent for the lots, and those who lived along one of the company's power or water lines could have electricity or water for the same charge.

Growth of the working-class in Joplin led to sporadic bursts of union activity but the district remained essentially unorganized until the Depression of the 1930s. As early as 1872, worker combines were organized to protect the interests of self-employed lease operators against the high royalty rates charged by land companies. These groups played a part in the destruction of a Joplin smelter by forty or fifty masked gunmen on July 20, 1874. By the late 1880s the Knights of Labor were active in trying to organize local miners. While they did not succeed, the Knights did sponsor Joplin's first observance of Labor Day on September 6, 1886.

After 1900 organized labor became more active and in May of that year workers successfully struck the Granby company mines at Oronogo, demanding that wage raises be tied to the sharp increases in ore prices. Shortly after this a flurry of labor unrest swept the mining fields over enforcement of the eight-hour-day labor law. From this time until 1915, most of the labor agitation came from the local chapters of the Industrial Workers of the World (IWW) which was then active in the mining fields of the West. This union had Socialist connections and the local Socialist party published the *Socialist News* at Carl Junction in 1906 and 1907. As part of the Labor Day festivities in 1909, the Carpenters and Jointers Union sponsored Eugene Debs, head of the IWW, to speak at Schifferdecker Park. The IWW promoted a series of labor disturbances that culminated in an attempted strike in 1915 by its 3,000 district members but operators closed the mines and broke the strike. This completely demoralized the strikers and the unions lost their power in the mine fields for the next twenty years. Of the twenty-six unions functioning in the district in 1916, not a single one represented miners.

An important factor in Joplin's continued dominance of mining was its growing role in the manufacturing of mining machinery. The low-grade, scattered ore deposits stimulated the development of rather specialized machines. The pioneer in this field was Harmany's Foundry and Machine Shop in Lone Elm, dating from the mid-1870s. Many of the leaders in manufacturing mining machinery apprenticed in Harmany's shop. Freeman's Foundry, later known as the United Iron Works, also became a leader in this area. Located at Fourteenth and Joplin streets, Freeman employed about 300 workers and was only one of eleven large foundries and machine shops in Joplin at this time.

Growth was not limited to mining machinery. By 1904 the expanding metropolis also had ten wholesale houses, six factories, a flour mill, and six banks among other businesses. In 1903 George Graves opened the Joplin Automobile Company, the first automobile agency in Joplin. Thirteen years earlier he had opened Joplin's first bicycle shop. Graves' agency, featuring Buick automobiles, was soon joined by dealers handling Overland, Ford, and other makes. In 1909 some 520 automobiles were registered in Joplin.

Joplin experienced its decade of most rapid growth in the 1890s. In that ten-year period the young city grew by a spectacular 161.7 percent, reaching a population of 26,023 in 1900. It was by far Missouri's most rapidly growing city. With the price of zinc rising sharply, 10,000 people poured into the city in the last two years of the century and a housing shortage reminiscent of the 1870s began to develop. Real estate doubled in value and south Joplin began to grow rapidly.

Numerous subdivisions were annexed in the twenty-year period ending in 1910. Among them were Blendville in 1892 and Chitwood and Villa Heights in 1908. In 1898 Blendville developer Thomas W. Cunningham deeded Cunningham Grove, an eight-acre tract, to the city. Cunningham Park (as it was named) became the nucleus of Joplin's public park system.

Civic improvements continued during this period. A sewage system was completed in 1891 and three years later a new Jasper County courthouse was constructed at Seventh and Virginia. In 1898 the city extended Seventh Street eastward from Kentucky Avenue to supplement Broadway and Fifth streets and Wall Street was opened across the Missouri Pacific tracks at Tenth Street to create a new traffic artery to the south.

Yet Joplin, like most other rapidly growing cities, was suffering from "growing pains." Much of the housing for miners was primitive and there were complaints about the lack of sidewalks, unpaved streets, and street crossings that flooded with mud after heavy rains.

The downtown business district got a new look in 1892 when E.Z. Wallower completed construction of the Keystone Hotel at the southeast corner of Fourth and Main streets. Six stories high and styled like a medieval castle, this was Joplin's first important high-rise building. Diagonally across Main Street Thomas Connor tore down the old Joplin Hotel in 1906 and built the even more magnificent Connor Hotel that towered eight stories above the street. Both of these hotels were landmarks on the Joplin skyline until about 1970.

Joplin featured many entertainment facilities by the turn of the century and was noted for the nightlife of its saloons, the most famous of which was the House of Lords, located on the east side of Main Street across from the Connor Hotel. Primarily a drinking place and a restaurant, contemporary reports claimed that gambling and prostitution went on in the upstairs rooms. Many prominent people frequented the House of Lords and mining en-

Facing page, top left: The Frisco Railroad office, at Sixth and Main, was photographed in 1904. Note the spitoon on the floor and the absence of women employees. Courtesy, Dorothea B. Hoover Historical Museum

Top right: This primitive automobile, known as the "Goat," is Joplin's claim to firefighting fame. Built by A.C. Webb on a Buick chassis in 1906 and purchased by the city in 1907, it was reportedly the first piece of motorized fire equipment in the nation. Equipped with a sixty-gallon chemical tank, 300 feet of hose, and two fire extinguishers, the Goat served until 1915 when it was dismantled for use as an inspection truck by the city electrician. Courtesy, Dorothea B. Hoover Historical Museum

Bottom: The New Method Steam Laundry, located at 213 West Fourth Street, was founded by C.A. Neil in 1897. The owner claimed he had the largest and most modern laundry in the Southwest. Note the horse-drawn delivery carts. Courtesy, Dorothea B. Hoover Historical Museum

trepreneurs often closed important business deals at its elegant tables while orchestras and bands played. The cafe, staffed with some of the best chefs in the Midwest, was known for its delicious steaks. Scott Joplin entertained here in 1896 as did two other prominent piano players: Thomas Greene "Blind Tom" Bethune and John W. "Blind Boone" Boone. The famed bistro closed in 1920 with the coming of Prohibition.

Main Street on Saturday nights during the heyday of the mining era was festive. Saturday marked the end of the six-day workweek and miners wages and the operators accounts for ore were paid at this time. Between 7 p.m. and 8 p.m. the banks were open and operators set up booths inside the banks or in saloons where they paid the miners. In that one-hour period over $100,000 was ordinarily disbursed. From 8 p.m. until midnight the stores and sidewalks were crowded with shoppers and with people socializing. Stores transacted about 25 percent of their week's business on these Saturday nights.

Joplin's black population increased slightly during this time. Few blacks were ever employed in the mines. Although some owned mining property and amassed considerable wealth, most worked as unskilled laborers and as servants.

A lynching and a race riot marred Joplin's history during this period. The last two decades of the nineteenth century were a time of growing racial tension in southwest Missouri. Feelings were running high in the spring of 1903. Two policemen had been murdered in less than a year. A black man had recently been lynched at Pierce City, and a series of burglaries had plagued Joplin stores. On April 14 policeman Theo Leslie discovered a gang of blacks occupying a boxcar in the railyards at the Kansas City Bottoms. While the policeman was attempting to search one of them, Thomas Gilyard, leader of the band, fired on the officer. The policeman turned to face his assailant and in the ensuing exchange of shots, Leslie fell dead. Gilyard fled with a bullet wound in the leg.

A great wave of excitement swept the town. Bloodhounds were brought in and posses scoured the countryside. The next day the limping Gilyard, carrying a gun, was sighted near Castle Rock.

With the prisoner lodged in the city jail, a crowd soon gathered. Frenzied men battered down the jail door and smashed the lock on Gilyard's cell with a sledgehammer. Borne away to Second and Wall streets on a bobbing sea of shoulders, the accused murderer seemed resigned to his fate. More rational men tried to reason with the mob. Attorney Perl Decker, hoisted on the shoulders of the crowd, made an eloquent plea to let the law take its course. Pulled down, Decker clambered back time and again, but the shouts drowned out his appeal. Mayor-elect Thomas Cunningham forced his buggy into the dense crowd but his appeal was also in vain. With Gilyard's clothes half torn away, a noose was fitted around his neck and as he was strung from a telephone pole three shots were fired into his body.

After Gilyard's body was taken to the morgue, the restless crowd began attacking homes of black residents, concentrating on the settlement located in the Kansas City Bottoms. Much destruction ensued and three houses were set on fire. When the fire department responded, the mob cut their water hoses. The next morning many blacks packed their belongings and left by train.

About 100 black families fled. Although most later returned, some never did. Among the latter appears to have been Langston Hughes' family. His father worked briefly as a stenographer for the Joplin Lead and Zinc Company. Langston Hughes later graduated from Lincoln University and wrote a number of books and Broadway plays. His novel, *Not Without Laughter,* won the Harmond award for literature. Following Hughes' death in 1967, Joplin citizens renamed a section of Broadway Boulevard after him.

Joplinites responded to the outbreak of the Spanish-American War in May 1898 with enthusiasm. A patent medicine advertisement in the *Joplin Herald* urged volunteers to condition themselves to withstand the "baneful Cuban climate" by taking "liberal and frequent doses of Prickly Ash Bitters." The local Company G, Second Infantry, of the Missouri National Guard experienced little difficulty in building up its complement of volunteers. A crowd of 5,000 cheered the volunteers as they boarded a special train at the Missouri Pacific depot only one week after the outbreak of war. The unit was assigned to the training camp at Chickamauga National Park, Georgia, where they remained until the end of the brief war. When Company G, headed by Captain Robert A. Spears, returned from its uneventful sojourn, a reception and banquet was held in its honor.

Joplin residents remained evenly split politically. In their first Presidential election in 1872 a majority of Joplinites voted for President Grant but by the early 1890s the Populist movement began to influence voters and in the strongly contested Presidential race of 1896, William Jennings Bryan, the Democratic-Populist candidate, received a majority of the vote. The most interesting political contest that Joplinites participated in was the election of Annie Baxter to the position of Jasper County Clerk. She was reportedly the first woman to hold public office in the United States.

Joplin's public services continued to expand rapidly at the turn of the century. The first section of a new high school at Fourth

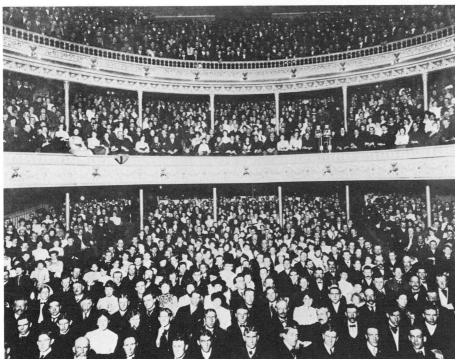

Above left: Annie Baxter White, a staunch Democrat elected Jasper County Clerk in 1890, is hailed in many accounts as the first woman in the U.S. to hold public office. Women were not allowed to vote at the time, but a peculiarity of Missouri law did not prevent them from holding office. A street in West Joplin is named after her. Courtesy, Carthage Press

Above right: St. John's Hospital was photographed soon after its completion in 1902. Located at Twenty-second and Connor, then at the edge of the city, it was built with funds raised by the Sisters of Mercy with Patrick Murphy donating the eight lots on which it was located for one dollar. Note the horse-drawn ambulance that was typical of the preautomotive age. Courtesy, Dorothea B. Hoover Historical Museum

Left: A capacity crowd of 1,400 attended the opening of the Club Theater on January 26, 1891, and watched a performance of "King Henry VIII." Erected by the Joplin Club at Fourth and Joplin, the building served a dual role as club house and theater. Courtesy, Dorothea B. Hoover Historical Museum

and Byers was constructed. The Joplin Business College, offering a full curriculum in bookkeeping and business education, was established in 1892. A movement to establish a public library got underway with the formation of the Public Library Association. When it became evident that popular subscriptions would not be enough, the association worked to secure passage of a library tax and this was accomplished in 1901, just in time to take advantage of a $40,000 donation by the philanthropist, Andrew Carnegie. The new Carnegie Library was completed at Ninth and Wall in 1902. In 1895 Joplin's first hospital, St. John's, was founded.

Fraternal societies and other private groups were also active in promoting the interests of the city. The Joplin Club strongly promoted civic affairs by bringing many conventions to Joplin as well as sponsoring construction of the Club Theater. Women took the lead in forming the city's first charitable organization, the Charitable Union, which helped the needy during the depression of 1893. In cold weather union members distributed coal and wood to the destitute living in box houses and tents in the Kansas City Bottoms. In 1899 the Joplin Children's Home was established as a refuge for homeless children.

The census of 1910 showed Joplin had a population of 32,073. Though not as spectacular as the growth of the 1890s, it was still substantial and enough to further solidify Joplin's position as the metropolis of the Tri-State mining district. Located within the ten-mile radius of Joplin were eleven towns, making an aggregate population, including Joplin, of over 80,000. These towns were tied to Joplin not only by roads and railways but also by an electric trolley system. Joplin's future as the capital of the district seemed assured.

The Elks hosted numerous social activities, including street fairs, to raise money. Such fairs usually began with a grand parade and thousands of people lined Main Street to see the flower-bedecked carriages and floats. This rig won first prize in the 1902 parade. Courtesy, Dorothea B. Hoover Historical Museum

Lakeside Park's dance pavilion was busy on
this evening in 1903. In addition to the pavilion, the park featured a hotel, boating and
swimming facilities, a theater, a baseball diamond, and midway attractions including a roller coaster. Courtesy, Dorothea B. Hoover
Historical Museum

CHAPTER FOUR

A Maturing Urban Center

In the two decades between 1910 and 1930 Joplin's growth slowed, but expansion of the area's interurban trolley system and construction of a modern highway network strengthened the young metropolis' ascendancy. As growth slowed and mining shifted away from the city's immediate environs, Joplin's population and the nature of its economic activities underwent a transformation that made the city a more mature and urbanized center.

An important shift in the locale of Tri-State mining operations took place in the World War I era. Ore production in the immediate Joplin district began to drop as early as 1906 and the exhaustion of high-grade ore deposits touched off an intense search for new mining fields in nearby Kansas and Oklahoma. In August 1914 a prospector's drill rig, mired in the mud in Ottawa County, Oklahoma, was used to drill a chance hole that opened up the Picher field, the richest body of lead and zinc ever discovered in the Tri-State district.

World War I began in Europe at the very time of the Picher discovery and the price of lead and zinc skyrocketed. Zinc reached a peak price of about $100 per ton in 1915 and lead prices were up to $130 per ton as late as 1917. These attractive prices gave a terrific boost to the industry but before the end of the war ore prices began to fall and they plummeted sharply under the impact of the recession of 1920-1921. Though prices eventually stabilized at about $40 for zinc and $80 for lead, they were sufficiently low to cause the industry to concentrate heavily on the rich new ore fields of Ottawa County, Oklahoma, and Cherokee County, Kansas.

The Tri-State mining industry reached its apex under the stimulus of the new Picher field. Of all the ore mined in the Tri-State area, the Picher field produced over 60 percent, the Webb City field 15 percent, and Joplin 9-1/2 percent. Districtwide production peaked in the years 1925 and 1926. The latter year saw the greatest tonnage—840,870 tons of zinc ore and 130,266 tons of lead—while the former year witnessed the highest value of production—$44,284,229 in zinc and $15,131,286 in lead. Four thousand railway cars loaded with ore left the district each week.

Mining was always a dangerous occupation and with the passing years the industry became more concerned about safety measures. In 1898 the *Joplin Herald,* reporting on the death of a

Facing page, left: These two men were at work in the Davey mine at Carterville circa 1915. Compressed air machines had replaced sledge hammers and hand steels for drilling blast holes and later models, like this example, sprayed water into the hole to prevent rock dust—a chief cause of silicosis. Courtesy, Tri-State Mineral Museum

Top right: Throughout Tri-State mining history, mules were the most widely used means of underground locomotion. Even after modern technology had established itself in most mines, many small operations still relied on mule power. The mules usually remained underground until death because their eyes were sensitive to sunlight. Courtesy, Tri-State Mineral Museum

Bottom right: This "man cage" at the Ballard mine in 1939 illustrates a growing awareness of needed safety measures. Previously, miners had been transported up and down the shafts in open ore cans and many men fell overboard. The hard hats were another safety innovation. Courtesy, Tri-State Mineral Museum

hoisterman, commented on the abominable safety record of the district's mines. Sixty miners had died in the first six months of the year, an average of one every three calendar days. In 1911 a Joplin miner, Joseph Clary, was buried alive by a mine cave-in. The disaster attracted nationwide attention but had a happy ending when rescuers freed him after a frantic seventy-two-hour effort. While miners faced the stark reality of sudden death in accidents, there were more subtle hazards that often eroded their health. The greatest health danger came from rock dust which caused silicosis and made the miners susceptible to tuberculosis.

About the time of World War I, stricter laws were passed concerning health and safety regulations. All these measures helped, but mining remained a hazardous occupation. In the late 1920s about twenty miners died each year from accidents, but the rate dropped to less than one-half this figure during the Depression.

In 1917 war broke out between the United States and Germany and Joplinites responded with the same patriotism that had been evident during the Spanish-American War. Even before America entered the war, its horror struck home on May 7, 1915, when prominent Joplin businessman, John Ferguson, lost his life when the British passenger liner, *Lusitania,* was sunk.

With the declaration of war on April 6, 1917, a giant loyalty parade moved down Main Street while a solemn crowd of thousands watched. Many area mines flew American flags. World War I, unlike the 1898 conflict, saw the imposition of a draft. On June 5 all men between the ages of twenty-one and thirty were required to register and 4,427 signed up that day. All the 3,700 men called into service were given a steak dinner at the House of Lords and escorted to the railway station by a band. Eighty-three Joplin men eventually lost their lives in the war.

Anti-German sentiment was noticeable during the war and prominent real estate broker, Adolph Schoenherr, changed his name to Dolph Shaner. He told the court that his obviously German name had become "a hindrance and an embarrassment."

Four liberty loan drives to sell war bonds were huge successes. They involved full-page advertisements in the newspapers and rallies on the vacant lot at Fourth and Main which became known as Liberty Lot.

Armistice Day, November 11, 1918, touched off a massive celebration. Crowds from all over the district began gathering in the morning and remained until night. Mayor Osborne asked the stores to close and observe a holiday. The thousands of revelers beat on old buckets, anvils, pieces of sheet metal, and bass drums and organized a parade in the afternoon.

The celebration took place despite an influenza epidemic that gripped the city. Some seventy-three people had died since the outbreak began early in October. Schools, theaters, and churches had been closed for nearly five weeks but with the crisis beginning to ease, city officials lifted the ban four days after the armistice.

A legacy of World War I was passage of the Eighteenth (Prohibition) Amendment. In 1887 the state legislature passed a local option law giving Missouri counties the power to declare themselves dry by a majority vote, though municipalities with a population of 2,500 or more were given the right to vote independently on the issue. Jasper County and Carthage immediately declared themselves dry, but the sentiment in Joplin was so negative that the issue did not even come up for a vote. In the fall of 1909, after a gigantic revival meeting by the famed temperance evangelist, "Billy" Sunday, the dry group forced a city-wide referendum on prohibition, but the issue failed and Joplin remained wet. By 1919, when Prohibition was ratified, Joplin stood as a wet oasis in a dry area that encompassed all the counties of southwest Missouri and the adjoining areas of Kansas and Oklahoma. As a result, Joplin was the regional center for an extensive bootleg business that further added to the city's reputation as a rough mining camp.

The Volstead Act, passed by Congress to implement the Eighteenth Amendment, stated that all liquor sales must end by January 16, 1920. On the day before Prohibition went into effect, the three Joplin chapters of the Women's Christian Temperance Union held jubilee celebrations while dejected saloon owners were busy taking down their signs. Liquor interests reported sales had been heavy for several days and supplies were depleted as customers stocked up for the long drought ahead. Bootleg liquor (Ozark White Mule) also began to rise steadily in demand as well as in price. Few of the city's fifty-two saloons were able to make the transition to another line of business. Owners of the House of Lords tried to carry on as a restaurant, but in January 1922, shortly after moving to 407 Main Street, it was closed.

A key factor in Joplin's ability to maintain its position as the district's urban center was the elaborate interurban trolley system that linked the city to the most important mineral areas. Prior to 1890 Joplin had depended on mule-car lines for public transportation, but in that year the Joplin Electric Street Railway Company installed an electric trolley line between East Joplin and downtown, which was later extended to Blendville.

At about the same time, Alfred H. Rogers, a Springfield businessman, established a mule-car line between Webb City and Carterville. With the advent of electric streetcars, Rogers assembled

Facing page, top left: Elizabeth Offutt Brown, founder of Joplin's first kindergarten, is seen here with her 1913 class at the Columbia School. Mrs. Brown (seated at the back table) decorated the blackboards with artwork. Bob Cummings, who later became a distinguished actor, was a member of this class but is not in the photo. Courtesy, Virginia Brown Weida

Top right: The Horseshoe Cafe, located at 315 Main, was one of Joplin's most popular restaurants in the early 1900s. As seen on the menu, a Porterhouse steak cost thirty-five cents. Courtesy, Dorothea B. Hoover Historical Museum

Bottom: When this photo was taken circa 1915, T.W. Osterloh operated two stores, one at 312 Main and this one at 804 Main. His business was the best known and most long-lived of its kind, dealing in books, stationery, office supplies, cameras, and recreational equipment. Courtesy, Dorothea B. Hoover Historical Museum

an extensive interurban trolley system known as the Southwest Missouri Railroad Company.

By 1907 Rogers' elaborate trolley system served most of the mining districts, but he encountered strong competition from J.J. Heim who was promoting his new Joplin and Pittsburg Railway Company. The Heim line extended westward from downtown to Schifferdecker Park and on to Pittsburg. Heim, who had the support of Gilbert Barbee, owner of the *Joplin Globe,* hoped to expand his line in Joplin but both men ran into the determined oppositon of Rogers. The latter bought control of the *Globe* and forced out Barbee, who had regularly savaged the Webb City railway executive in the columns of his newspaper. Then Rogers bought heavily into the Pittsburg railway, compelling Heim to abandon his plans for expansion although his thirty-five-mile system continued to operate between Joplin, Pittsburg, and intermediate towns.

The Rogers line expanded as demand developed and remained prosperous for many years. Fares for in-city travel were five cents. A Joplin-to-Picher journey cost fifty-five cents. Approximately 90 percent of the line's business came from miners who could be seen clinging to the outside of the pea-green cars during rush hours. Gross volume peaked at over one million dollars in 1918 and in 1919, but increased use of automobiles caused a decline in the 1920s.

By the 1920s miners were taking advantage of the new highways to go to work in car pools, then called "buddy cars." During the Depression the Southwest Missouri line replaced its streetcars with buses on the Joplin routes and the final trolley car passenger run was made between Galena and Picher on May 7, 1938.

But buses could not solve the Rogers line's revenue problems. Already insolvent, the beleaguered company announced early in 1939 that it was suspending city service. Faced with the prospect of a public transportation system limited to taxicabs, the city agreed to transfer the bus franchise to the Joplin Public Service Company, organized by W.M. Robertson. Robertson succeeded in maintaining limited service with a fleet of small, twenty-one passenger buses.

A major factor in Joplin consolidating its position as the district's urban center was the growth of a network of good roads outside the city limits. The Joplin Special Road District (JSRD) and John Malang, its superintendent from 1914 to 1928, played a leading role in these developments. Malang, who became a leading figure in developing Missouri's state road system, promoted the building of concrete roads utilizing local low-cost mine waste called chat. Under his jurisdiction eight such roads were built at a time when few concrete roads existed elsewhere.

By 1910 Joplin's railroad system had stablized and no more major lines were built into the city. In 1911 most of the railroads combined to build a new Union Station and the old passenger depots at Tenth and Main, and Fourth and Gulf were closed. Located just north of Broadway in the Joplin Creek valley on the site where Moffet and Sergeant had built Joplin's first lead smelter forty years earlier, the new depot was designed by the nationally known architect, Louis Curtiss. The Frisco Railroad, with a depot at Sixth and Virginia, chose not to join in the new project and instead completed an eight-story depot and office building in 1913 at Sixth and Main. Joplin's first high-rise office building, the Frisco edifice continues as a downtown landmark though it was abandoned as a passenger depot in the 1950s.

The census of 1920 showed Joplin with a population of 29,902, a drop of 2,171 people from the 1910 figure. This decline, the first official population drop in Joplin's history, undoubtedly resulted from the mining industry shifting to the new Picher field.

Despite the precipitate decline in mining in the immediate area, Joplin stablized its economy and experienced real growth and prosperity during the remainder of the 1920s. The city succeeded in this by becoming less dependent on mining and turning more to agriculture and tourism, a trend greatly facilitated by the automobile.

Rural areas, always important to Joplin, became more so as businessmen began to reach a much larger farm area. With the improved roads and Joplin's large home market, businessmen soon recognized that agriculture was becoming the Tri-State district's leading industry. Prior to World War I, Joplin newspapers paid little attention to agriculture. Starting about 1915 the *Joplin Globe*'s Sunday edition featured a page titled "Farm Department." On December 4, 1921, the *News Herald* added a monthly agricultural supplement. Commenting on this new feature, the editor noted that for years district leaders had concentrated on developing the mining industry while neglecting the growing importance of agriculture. At this time, the Joplin Chamber of Commerce worked with area farm organizations to promote fruit and truck growing and to get mining speculators to sell their land so it could be developed into farms.

Joplin business leaders also worked to promote tourism, and various towns and resorts in southwest Missouri and northwest Arkansas formed the Ozark Playgrounds Association, headquartered in Joplin, to coordinate this activity. Joplin was billed as the "Gateway to the Ozarks."

With Joplin's growing importance as a commercial center in

Top left: Strawberry pickers toiling in the hot sun were a common sight in the Joplin area circa 1915. More than one-half of Missouri's strawberries were produced in the five southwest Missouri counties clustered around Joplin. Years of heavy production required as many as 25,000 workers, and many of them were women and teenagers. The decline in mining brought the collapse of the strawberry industry due to a lack of pickers. Courtesy, State Historical Society of Missouri

Top right: This mangled wreckage was all that remained of a Missouri and North Arkansas rail car after its fiery head-on collision with a Kansas City Southern train at Tipton Ford. Forty-three people died in the crash on August 5, 1914, just twenty minutes after the rail car left Joplin's Union Station. Approximately 10,000 people attended a mass funeral service at Neosho for twenty-five of the victims who were burned beyond recognition. A monument in Neosho's I.O.O.F. Cemetery marks their grave. Courtesy, Dorothea B. Hoover Historical Museum

Above: The Boucher Cigar Company began in 1904 with five employees hand rolling five- and ten-cent cigars. By 1921 the work force numbered 175 and was mostly women. Boucher was one of several manufacturers that moved to Joplin to utilize the many female workers who could not find employment in the mines. Courtesy, Dorothea B. Hoover Historical Museum

the 1920s, business grew rapidly. Mine-related industries continued to be important and many highly specialized machines that enjoyed a worldwide market were designed and patented by Joplin firms. In 1927 the two largest firms, the United Iron Works and Rogers Foundry, merged and the new firm continued under the leadership of C.B. Rogers. Joplin also had three explosives manufacturers that catered to the heavy demand for dynamite to shatter rock formations in the mines.

The area's business became much more diversified during the 1920s. By 1925 the city had 141 manufacturing establishments with Eagle-Picher being the largest. This concern employed about 700 workers in manufacturing lead-based materials. Agriculture-related industries included grain mills, feed processing plants, packing establishments, and creameries.

Joplin's busy downtown shopping district was dominated by three department stores. The Newman Store had been established in 1898. In 1910 the firm built a new five-story building at Sixth and Main. The Christman Dry Goods Company, dating back to 1890, completed a new five-story building at Fifth and Main in 1918. The third department store, Ramsay's, opened in 1910 and its three-story building was located at Sixth and Main.

Other construction projects that marked Joplin's progress in the 1920s were the Scottish Rite Cathedral, the First Baptist Church, and the South Joplin Christian Church. A $750,000 school bond, issued in 1926, resulted in the building of a new South Joplin Junior High School and a new Irving Elementary School. A new four-story addition to St. John's Hospital was completed in 1927. In 1922 Freeman Hospital was founded with the gift of a house at Twentieth and Sergeant by Mr. and Mrs. John W. Freeman. Downtown construction also included completion of a new wing on the Connor Hotel in 1929. Rooms in this annex rented for two to three dollars a day. New housing subdivisions continued to open up, particularly in south Joplin. The price for a five-room house was between $2,000 and $5,000 in the 1920s.

As Joplin's downtown business district matured, it was characterized by a few colorful figures who enlivened the district's routine workday activities. One of these personalities was "Colonel" Jimmy Worth. A cab driver, Worth married a wealthy widow who owned the building at the northeast corner at Fourth and Main that later bore his name. A true eccentric, Worth's appearance made him one of the most memorable characters to frequent Joplin. He often was attired in plaid suits and flashy ties with a large diamond stickpin. Several electric light bulbs, which he flashed with a switch, were attached to the toes of his shoes and sometimes to his vests. If his electrical display did not attract enough attention, Jimmy was known on occasion to light a cigar with a $20 bill. Equally eccentric was the horse man who became a common sight on Main Street early in the century. Evidently aspiring to be a horse, he shod his boots with horseshoes and pulled a wagon, basking in the attention of onlookers.

As Joplin matured it became a more cultured city and produced a few figures who rose to national prominence in the entertainment field. Some music historians believe Joplin played an important role in the development of ragtime music and this connection is evident with Percy Wenrich who was born in the mining city in 1880. Wenrich's talents developed early. As a sixteen-year-old he once hid behind a screen in the House of Lords to hear Scott Joplin play the piano. Known as the "Joplin Kid," Percy became popular and toured the vaudeville circuit for fifteen years with his wife, Dolly Connolly. Wenrich is best remembered for such ragtime tunes as "When You Wore a Tulip," "On Moonlight Bay," and "Put on Your Old Gray Bonnet." The reference to Dover in the latter song refers to a hill in Joplin west of Ozark Bible College. Wenrich died in 1952 and is buried in Fairview Cemetery.

Motion pictures, which were new about the time of World War I, slowly replaced traditional theater performances. Most showed a combination of pictures and vaudeville, though by 1927 theaters like the Rex and the New Theater showed only motion pictures. Joplin's largest theater, the Hippodrome, seated 2,000 people.

Sports activities, which earlier had been mostly horse and foot races, turned to baseball and golf in the 1920s. The Joplin Miners baseball team, long a member of the Western Association League, was formed early in the century. Joplinite Charles "Gabby" Street, who once managed the Miners, later headed the St. Louis Cardinals and led them to a World Series championship. A boulevard in Joplin is named after him. The Miners were long a farm team for the New York Yankees, and Yankee star Mickey Mantle, who grew up in the area, got his start with the veteran Joplin team.

Not the least of Joplin's recreational attractions was its splendid public park system which by the mid-1920s encompassed about 500 acres. Beginning with Cunningham Park in 1896, this system expanded steadily to include Roanoke Park in northwest Joplin, Leonard Park in Villa Heights, Mineral Park at Galena and Pool streets, Ewert Park in East Joplin, Schifferdecker Park at the west end of Fourth Street and three parks located on Shoal Creek: McClelland, McIndoe, and Witmer. Schifferdecker was the most highly developed. Built originally as an amusement park, it was known as the Electric Park until its developer, Charles Schifferdecker, bequeathed it to the city in 1913. Encompassing

160 acres, it featured the finest eighteen-hole golf course in the district. Horton Smith and other professionals played there in the 1920s, at which time the fee was twenty-five cents per day.

Women began to play an important role in Joplin politics even before they gained the vote nationally in 1920. In the school board election of 1918, two women, Mrs. Helen Donehoo and Mrs. Emma Sellers Hill, entered the contest. Mrs. Hill lost, but Mrs. Donehoo won and became the first woman to hold elective office in Joplin.

In the early 1920s the Ku Klux Klan, experiencing a revival in the aftermath of World War I, became active in Joplin politics. It is difficult to trace the activities of the Klan in Joplin between 1921 and 1923, the years of its greatest power. Local newspapers gave it little coverage, but the Klan was influential in the 1922 municipal election and probably brought about the defeat of Mayor Jesse P. Osborne and Police Commissioner Joe H. Myers, who refused to permit the Klansmen to parade hooded in the city. The Klan had its "Klavern," or meeting place, in a cave north of the city. Some important individuals in Joplin were briefly associated with the Klan and it posed a threat to Catholics and Jews as well as blacks.

As the end of the 1920s approached, civic boosters were ecstatic about Joplin's future. They indeed had much to praise. The decrease in population had been reversed and the census of 1930 showed a count of 33,454, an increase of 3,552 over the 1920 figure. A significant part of the increase came from incorporating the suburbs of Freeman Grove, Stapleton, Dunwoody, Hatten, Castle Rock, and Royal Heights. Joplin's city limits at the end of the decade ran approximately from Range Line on the east to a point one mile west of Schifferdecker Avenue and from County Line Road (32nd Street) on the south to Turkey Creek on the north.

Most Joplinites saw the transition to a more diversified economy as a good thing. It enabled the city to overcome its rough mining camp image. Most of the old two-room shacks had been razed and replaced with better housing. The population, no longer transitory, consisted of trades people, laborers, and professionals and city officials optimistically predicted a population increase of 12,000 over the next ten years.

CHAPTER FIVE

Depression, War, and Readjustment

Jasper mine, located west of Joplin, was one of the mines that opened up in abandoned ore fields during World War II. Recovery of the low-grade ore was made possible by government subsidies. In this 1944 photo the crew is proud of their safety record and their contribution to the war effort. Courtesy, Tri-State Mineral Museum

The optimistic forecasts of a decade of rapid growth for Joplin were blighted by the onset of the Great Depression in 1929, but even with continued prosperity the city's expansion would have been slowed by exhaustion of the high-grade lead and zinc deposits in the Tri-State district.

Lead and zinc prices slumped drastically during the Depression. In November 1929 zinc concentrate sold for $42 per ton and lead for $80 per ton. By mid-1932 prices reached a low of approximately $18 for zinc and $32.50 for lead concentrates. In 1931 smelters and many mines began to close as the industry struggled to dispose of surplus stock during 1932.

The effect on employment in the mines was catastrophic. From an all-time peak of 11,187 in 1924, employment dropped to as low as 500 part-time workers in the grim days of June and July 1932. After that, employment climbed slowly to an average of about 3,500 in 1935 though many were working part-time and earning only about $15 per week.

World War II relieved the Tri-State mining industry of the burden of depression, but did not solve all its problems. Once the United States entered the war, the new Office of Price Administration imposed a ceiling of $55.28 per ton on zinc concentrates and $76.20 on lead. These prices changed little throughout the war, but a system of government premiums, set up to encourage the mining of marginal deposits, raised the maximum price of zinc to $144.38 and lead to $159.80.

Under the stimulus of these wartime subsidies, the industry struggled to increase production but industry leaders were painfully aware that the great Tri-State fields were unprofitable after nearly 100 years of mining.

The onset of the Depression brought a surge of labor unionization. The unemployment and new labor legislation passed under the New Deal administration provided the catalyst that led to the unionization of the mine fields. The International Union of Mine, Mill, and Smelter Workers—affiliated with the American Federation of Labor (AFL)—began a unionization drive and on May 8, 1935, struck the mine fields. The Tri-State Ore Producers Association countered this movement by organizing a company union known as the Tri-State Metal Workers Union, popularly called the Blue Card Union. The Blue Card Union rallied a back-to-work movement that soon broke the strike and used "strong-arm" methods to frustrate the organizing efforts of the International Union until a 1938 ruling under the Wagner Labor Relations Act put an end to company union activities. Triumphant, the International Union, by then affiliated with the Congress of Industrial Organizations (CIO), became the sole union of the mining district.

While the miners were generally affiliated with the CIO, most unions in Joplin by the time of World War II were associated with the AFL. This union first became active during construction of the Keystone Hotel in the early 1890s when it moved to unionize the carpenters. Turning to other crafts, the AFL organized the Joplin Typographical Union in 1899. By 1942 other active locals were the Construction and General Laborers Union, General Drivers and Helpers Union, Carpenters Local, International Molders and Foundry Workers, and the United Garment Workers of America.

Joplin suffered severely from the Depression, but the city's diversified economy provided something of a cushion. Retail trade held up reasonably well as did agriculture-related industries. The years 1931 and 1932, before the advent of federal government relief programs, were the worst. The unemployed fared as best they could. Landlords were lenient about unpaid rent. Some unemployed moved in with relatives while others left for California, many never to return. The truly destitute built shacks out of scrap materials on abandoned mining company lands. The Provident Association, a local charitable organization, held fundraising drives and always stood ready to help those in dire need. Yet people found reasons to rejoice. New Year's Eve 1932 was a particularly festive occasion as people said farewell to 1931. The American Legion hosted a dance at Memorial Hall while the Paramount Theater presented a stage revue called "Hits and Misses of 1931."

Construction remained slow in 1932 but began to pick up in 1933 with the implementation of New Deal relief projects. One of the first of these was a Civil Works Administration (CWA) project to improve Landreth Park. W.H. Landreth had deeded the city 101 acres in the old Kansas City Bottoms. Sometimes known as Sunshine Hollow, the region rapidly deteriorated once mining ended in the vicinity. By early 1934 some 300 workmen were busy cleaning away the refuse and brush as well as cutting a boulevard through the area. The boulevard was a segment of a projected thoroughfare that would encircle the city. Promoted by the manager of the Joplin Special Road District, Howard Murphy, the section from north Main Street through Landreth Park to

Facing page, left: The Great Depression brought increased gouging in the Joplin area as unemployed miners tried to eke out a living by reworking old diggings. Their equipment was often primitive as indicated in this photo of a gouger operating a hand windlass, reminiscent of those used in the 1870s. Courtesy, Tri-State Mineral Museum

Top right: Many old miner's shacks located in abandoned mine fields were occupied by destitute families during the Great Depression. These shacks, which were primitive at best, became hovels as the years passed. An old car was always useful for transportation if the owner could afford to buy gasoline and decrepit Model T Fords, as seen here, could be purchased for fifteen to twenty-five dollars. Courtesy, Dorothea B. Hoover Historical Museum

Bottom right: Shown here is the Oronogo Circle mine in 1945. Claimed to be the world's largest open-pit lead mine at that time, it was also one of the few strip-pit mines in the Tri-State district. A reported thirty million dollars worth of ore has been taken from this rich sinkhole deposit which is up to 240 feet deep. Courtesy, Tri-State Mineral Museum

Displaying the boyish grin that helped make him one of the great popular heroes of the 1920s, Charles A. Lindbergh is shown here with his wife, Anne Morrow Lindbergh, during a stopover in Joplin in early 1930. A few months after this flight Mrs. Lindbergh gave birth to a son, Charles Augustus, Jr., the couple's first child. Twenty months later the youngster was murdered in a brutal kidnapping. Courtesy, Dorothea B. Hoover Historical Museum

Twelfth Street (later renamed Murphy Boulevard) was completed at this time.

Other projects were undertaken in late 1933 and 1934 using CWA funds, including construction of Junge Stadium, and in 1935 the CWA was replaced with the Works Progress Administration (WPA), a greatly expanded program that provided jobs for the unemployed. The Seventh District WPA headquarters was located in Joplin and extensive projects were undertaken in the city including paving, removal of streetcar tracks, lighting, and viaduct construction. Other projects involved park improvements, school construction, sidewalk repairs, and installation of storm sewers.

Another important WPA project was the development of Joplin's airport. Lincoln Beechy flew the first airplane in Joplin during an exhibition over the Schifferdecker Electric Park about 1910, but it was not until 1927 that a flying field designated as the Joplin Municipal Airport was opened. This field consisted of 160 acres just south of the Schifferdecker golf course between Seventh and Thirteenth streets. Rented by the chamber of commerce, it was dedicated with an air show in November of that year. In 1935 the city purchased 319 acres of land two miles north of town. Located adjacent to the Harper flying school, this track became the nucleus of Joplin's present-day airport. Between 1935 and 1937 WPA projects included construction of three gravel runways, an apron, and lights. In 1942 the Civil Aeronautics Authority allocated $365,000 to pave two 4,250-foot runways and install improved drainage and lighting to serve the new military base at Camp Crowder. After World War II, taking advantage of federal grants, the city improved the runways and added an administration building. At this time Mid-Continent and American Airlines offered regularly scheduled passenger flights in and out of the airport.

The largest WPA project in the district involved draining the 5,000-acre mining field of Oronogo-Webb City-Carterville in 1937. Up to 750 workers were employed in building canals to channel the water into Center Creek. Soon nearly 300 miners were once again at work in the fields, but the business recession of 1938 caused a cutback and water soon reclaimed most of the mines.

Joplin's black population of approximately 900 continued to make slow progress. At an earlier time, when blacks were denied access to the public parks, there were few places where they could meet in large numbers, but on August 4 of each year they celebrated Emancipation Day at Schifferdecker Park. In 1924, Paul H. Ewert, a local lawyer and mine operator, deeded 11.45 acres to establish a park for Joplin's blacks.

Though suffering from the privations of the Depression, they shared in the benefits of the WPA and most were able to find jobs, but only at subsistence wages. Many black-owned businesses also sprang up to serve the local black community.

The early years of the Depression spawned an increase in crime that caused nationwide alarm. This new brand of criminal used the automobile as an escape vehicle and Joplin, with its excellent network of highways, became a favorite hideout of outlaws. Some of the more notorious who hid in Joplin were the Barker gang led by the indomitable "Ma" Barker, "Pretty Boy" Floyd, and the Barrow gang of whom the most famous were Clyde Barrow and Bonnie Parker. In the spring of 1933 the Barrow gang killed two law enforcement officers in a shootout in Freeman Grove. The battle brought Joplin nationwide publicity and touched off an intense search for the criminals.

The end of Prohibition in 1933 helped quiet this era of lawlessness. On August 11, 1933, Joplinites voted to elect delegates to a constitutional convention that would either ratify or reject the Twenty-first Amendment to repeal Prohibition. Delgates favoring repeal won, but all the counties adjacent to Jasper voted against repeal. With Prohibition repealed, the city commission adopted an ordinance legalizing the sale of liquor by the drink, but prohibited such establishments from using the term "saloon." Joplin soon had a number of bars as they now came to be called.

Though there were many Depression-related bankruptcies, some businesses continued to expand and this was due chiefly to Joplin's growing importance as a highway transportation center. The early years of the Depression touched off an extensive highway building program and Joplin became the junction of two major interstate routes: Highway 66 and Highway 71. Local boosters termed the city the "Crossroads of America" and it became widely known as an important center in the growing commerce that flowed through the city by automobile, bus, and truck. This was further augmented by a reference to Joplin in a hit song about "Route 66."

The stimulus of these new routes was obvious. Twenty motor freight lines and several bus companies operated in and out of Joplin. Tourist courts sprang up, located mostly along Seventh Street on the route of Highway 66, and presaging the future intense commercial development of that traffic artery, new industries began to appear along Range Line, the route of Highway 71 bypass. The greatest effect was on agriculture-related industries and this resulted in two of the most important commercial developments during the 1930s: construction of the stockyards and ex-

This apartment at Thirty-fourth and Oak Ridge has changed little since April 14, 1933, when it was the site of a gun battle between law officers and Clyde and Buck Barrow, Buck's wife, Blanche, and Bonnie Parker. After killing two policemen, the criminals fled east on Thirty-fourth to Main and then south on Main. Courtesy, Dewayne L. Tuttle

pansion of the City Market.

The growth of milk plants and creameries, and the establishment of three meat-packing plants highlighted the area's growing importance as a dairy and beef-cattle region. This, accompanied by an expanding highway system, made Joplin an ideal center for a livestock market. In 1931 promoters capitalized on the opportunity by building the Joplin Stockyards. Designed to facilitate the loading and unloading of trucks, it also had railroad connections. Conceived as a regional market, the yards aimed particularly at bringing northwestern Arkansas into the Joplin market sphere. Promoters of the new yards pictured Joplin as a four-state trading center. The stockyards also strengthened retail sales because farmers often stayed to shop after selling their cattle. The yards were a resounding success from the start despite being opened in the very depths of the Depression. In the first five years of operation, they handled a little over one million head of livestock and paid fifteen million dollars to area farmers.

Joplin's highway connections and the growth of an important local fruit industry also stimulated expansion of the City Market. This market had long existed on a small scale but had been unprofitable. Joe H. Myers, Commissioner of Public Property and Public Utilities, sensed the growth potential of the market as a truck-in center and succeeded in getting a building completed in 1935 to house the operation. Located at Twelfth and Virginia, it rapidly became a leading regional exchange wholesale market. By the end of the decade about 40,000 trucks from forty states, Mexico, and Canada were using the market each year.

Joplin continued to mature as a cultural and civic center during the 1930s. Mrs. Jay L. Wilder was a leading promoter of cultural events in the city. Starting with a performance by Fritz Kreisler, she brought many internationally known concert artists to Joplin including Nelson Eddy, Grace Moore, Marion Anderson, Lily Pons, and Lawrence Tibbet. During World War II, when big name artists were unavailable, she organized and promoted a symphony orchestra.

Other cultural activities were provided by the Joplin Little Theatre, which was founded in 1939 (and has since produced over 500 plays), and by radio station WMBH. Established in 1926, it remained Joplin's only station through World War II.

The Tri-State Mineral Museum was an important addition to the city's cultural attractions. Joe H. Myers saw the need to preserve the district's mining heritage and with J.H. Wadleigh and Fred H. Nesbitt he formed the first museum board which acquired the old building in Schifferdecker Park. After soliciting $200,000 from district mine operators to remodel the building and set up exhibits, Myers opened the museum in 1931.

An event most Joplinites looked forward to during the Depression era was the Fiesta Days celebration held each April. Sponsored by the chamber of commerce to stimulate downtown retail business, events included a carnival and a colorful evening parade and culminated in a prize drawing. To get into the spirit, many people wore fiesta costumes and Spanish hats, as did clerks in the stores. Merchants distributed tickets for the drawing, which had a grand prize of $500, with each purchase. A massive crowd always gathered at Sixth and Main where the drawing was held.

Civic services continued to expand during the difficult Depression years, though at a reduced pace. The city's third hospital, the Joplin General Osteopathic Hospital, opened in August 1937 at Fourth and Moffet. In 1963 the institution, renamed the Oak Hill Osteopathic Hospital, moved to East Thirty-fourth Street.

The most important development in the field of education in the 1930s was the establishment of Joplin Junior College. It opened in 1937 as an extension of the University of Missouri. Classes were held at the senior high school the first year and the next fall the college moved into the newly remodeled North Junior High School. The school had an enrollment of 335 and the first class of twenty-four graduated in the spring of 1939. By then it was the third largest junior college in Missouri.

Between 1935 and 1940 business showed a decisive upturn in Joplin except for a temporary slump during the recession of 1938. The outbreak of war in Europe in September 1939 added a strong stimulus to the recovery of Joplin's economy.

The census of 1940 showed Joplin with a population of 37,144, up 11 percent from 1930. Though the economic reverses of the Depression were severe, the city had made a strong comeback by the end of the decade. The census showed the population to be 96.8 percent native white, one percent foreign-born white, and 2.2 percent black. The racial composition had varied little in the city's history.

When the Japanese attacked Pearl Harbor, Joplinites were subdued. There were no parades as at the outbreak of World War I, but young men felt a patriotic call to duty and on December 8 enlistees crowded the military recruiting offices. The press of enlistees became so great that the office remained open until midnight. A fear of sabotage gripped public officials and all workers at Camp Crowder near Neosho were required to have passes. Guards were posted at the Joplin airport and at bridges on state and national highways in the district. The governor ordered all towns in Missouri to take steps to guard their water supplies. Though fears were eventually calmed, the need for security pre-

Left: Crystal Cave, a giant calcite-lined cavity, was discovered in 1894 at Fourth and Gray. Electric lights were installed and a dance floor and boardwalks were constructed so groups could hold meetings and parties in its cool recesses. Courtesy, Tri-State Mineral Museum

Below: A high school marching band leads Joplin's Fiesta Days parade at Sixth and Main on April 24, 1940. The huge crowd was typical of the throngs attracted by these festivities each year between 1935 and 1941. Note the people wearing Spanish hats, a tradition on Fiesta Days. Courtesy, Baird Studios

cautions led to the organization of a Civil Defense Agency and a Civil Air Patrol in Joplin.

The war affected life in Joplin in many ways. Unemployment, which had plagued the city for more than a decade, quickly disappeared. But more than anything else, wartime rationing presented an entirely new experience. The first items to be rationed were automobile tires and inner tubes. To prolong the life of tires, a speed limit of forty miles per hour, later reduced to thirty-five, was imposed. Other rationed items were new cars, bicycles, typewriters, rubber boots, and shoes.

Sugar was rationed in the spring of 1942. This required the first nationwide registration of every man, woman, and child ever undertaken. Nearly 43,000 people registered through the Joplin office and were issued books of "sugar stamps." Each person was limited to one-half pound of sugar per week with occasional bonus allotments and extra sugar allowed for canning. Coffee was added to the food list in November 1942 with each person over age fifteen limited to one pound every five weeks.

A heavy blow fell in December 1942 when, in an attempt to save tires, the Office of Price Administration (OPA) ordered the rationing of gasoline and fuel oil even though Midwest oilfields were overflowing with crude oil. Joplin's 8,000 motorists received "A" coupon books limiting them to four gallons each week. Rationing was accepted in good grace by most Joplinites because it seemed essential to the war effort but fuel oil rationing, which limited households to about one-half their normal supply, brought serious protests because of the abundant supply available.

Gasoline rationing did more to modify people's lifestyles than any other wartime restriction. Many abandoned driving to work in favor of public transportation, car pools, bicycles, or even walking. Nightclubs suffered heavily and large social gatherings were largely eliminated as people spent more evenings at home reading or listening to the radio. Business deliveries to homes were curtailed sharply and some, like milk routes, were never fully resumed after the war.

The Joplin area had an unusually large number of skilled workers in the mechanical arts because of the many jobs in mining and related industries that fostered these talents. Recognizing this, the federal government established an important defense training school in July 1940 to instruct workers in aircraft sheet metal work, welding, forging, and other related activities. Operated by the Joplin public school system in the Lafayette School annex, it provided free training to more than 8,000 workers during the war. After the war the Joplin R-8 School District continued this program of vocational training at its Franklin Technical School, which has long been regarded as one of the finest schools of its type.

The large numbers of soldiers stationed at Camp Crowder had an important effect on life in wartime Joplin. On any day of the week hundreds of uniformed personnel could be seen in the downtown business district and on weekends thousands of soldiers descended on the city seeking amusement and recreation. Local families were encouraged to invite a serviceman for dinner or to adopt one for a holiday weekend. The United Service Organization (USO) also set up an extensive social center for military personnel. Operated by volunteer women, it had a main lounge, kitchen, auditorium, serving room, and club rooms. Soldiers and USO girls frequently gathered there for Saturday night dances.

Unlike World War I, the Second World War ended in stages. President Truman proclaimed May 8, 1945, as V-E Day ending the war in Europe. Joplinites remained calm. Mayor Temples ordered the stores, bars, and schools closed and the downtown district experienced possibly the quietest day since the war began. Mindful that the war still continued against Japan, many people attended thanksgiving services at churches. The next day an official brownout ended and neon signs, window displays, and ornamental lights were turned on once again.

Joplin's citizens were less restrained on August 14 when President Truman announced that Japan had surrendered. The announcement came at 6 p.m. and carloads of celebrants immediately headed for downtown. Japanese Premier Tojo was hung in effigy from a traffic light at Fourth and Main while a cheering crowd of thousands blocked traffic. The bars were ordered closed and most other businesses also shut down, allowing the celebrants to take over the downtown area.

Joplinites were proud of their role in World War II. Through their defense-related industries, they had made a solid contribution to the war effort. Approximately 5,000 Joplin servicemen had served in the armed forces and 166 had lost their lives.

Joplin underwent a trying economic readjustment at the end of the war. The closing of Camp Crowder and the cancellation of defense contracts eliminated many jobs, but the tremendous pent-up purchasing power in the hands of consumers kept the retail trade strong and the resumption of the production of civilian goods added new jobs. Mining also remained important to Joplin's economy. As late as 1948 the Tri-State mine fields still employed approximately 5,000, but as the decade ended the mining industry began to slump.

The period from 1946 to 1950 saw a massive increase in construction. The housing industry boomed. Two new sewer plants, one on Turkey Creek and the other on Shoal Creek, were completed. The highway department completed a new viaduct on East Seventh at Range Line and began widening the former to four lanes. Southwestern Bell Telephone Company completed a new headquarters building and the Junge Baking Company began construction of a new biscuit and cracker plant.

During the 1940s Joplin seemed to be on an economic roller coaster as it rode the crest of a wartime boom in the first half of the decade only to have it collapse after 1945. But the result was positive. The pall of depression had lifted from the city and extensive construction changed the face of the municipality. The official census of 1950 showed a population of 38,711, up 4.2 percent from 1940, but the modest increase portended a major crisis in the mining industry.

This photo shows Vernon Sigars' "Band-wagon" at Schifferdecker Park during the congressional campaign of 1940. Sigars used the vehicle, built on an old ambulance chassis, to campaign throughout the district. The musicians were local high school boys. An underdog, Sigars lost to the incumbent Dewey Short. Courtesy, Vernon Sigars

CHAPTER SIX

New Horizons

This view looking southwest across Joplin and Wall avenues shows the large expanses cleared by urban renewal. Photo by G.K. Renner.

World War II had boosted Joplin's economy but that stimulus merely postponed the painful period of readjustment as the mines began to close. Turning from its mining past, the city was forced to seek new horizons to maintain its population and its position as the cultural and economic center of the Tri-State district. The predominant theme of the period from 1950 to 1980 is how Joplin met that challenge.

The Tri-State mining industry suffered its first major post-World War II crisis in 1949. That year brought an all-time high price of $292.17 per ton for lead concentrates and $110 for zinc. By the end of the year prices had fallen almost 50 percent. Operators blamed the decline on Marshall Plan economic aid to foreign competitors, but other contributing factors were the devaluation of foreign currencies and a series of strikes in industries that were major users of zinc and lead. A complete shutdown of the mining district seemed at hand, but experts warned that if the pumps stopped, the mines would be lost permanently because the underground was so heavily cut out that once the drifts flooded, the cost of dewatering would be prohibitive. Mine operators demanded that the workers accept wage cuts. Faced with this demand, the laborers struck and the mines were closed through most of July until Eagle-Picher, setting a pattern for the industry, negotiated a contract under which the miners returned to work at a pay cut of $3.08 per day. By fall, the large mines were back in operation although many small ones remained closed. The uncertain future of the mining industry received a temporary boost from the outbreak of the Korean War in June 1950. Ore prices immediately recovered and in 1951 they peaked at $135 per ton for zinc concentrates and $246.50 for lead. Still, most of the small operations remained closed due to skyrocketing labor costs.

Clearly, the industry was failing. Operators clamored for either increased tariff duties on foreign ore or a return to government subsidies as in World War II, but federal policy was equivocal. By 1951 a shortage of zinc existed in American industry and the supply of lead remained tight. As a means of stockpiling these strategic materials, the Federal Defense Materials Procurement Agency contracted with Tri-State producers to buy their output at a fixed price for up to two years. At the same time, this agency agreed to pay certain major foreign producers six cents a pound above the prevailing United States market price for zinc and lead concentrates. American markets were soon flooded with foreign ore and by mid-1953 zinc concentrate was selling for $65 per ton and lead for $154.74 per ton. The Tri-State district was paralyzed. A strike in late 1953 against Eagle-Picher closed most of the mines for six months. After this the crippled industry slowly ebbed away and by the 1960s all significant mining had ceased.

The Tri-State district has much to be proud of in its mining legacy. It stands as one of the most impressive developments in mining history. During a 125-year period more than 500 million tons of ore were taken from the ground. Bureau of Mines statistics show that the district produced 22,759,979 tons of zinc concentrate and 3,755,387 tons of lead. These concentrates had a contemporary value of $1,491,751,630 at the mines, and when converted by the smelters into refined ore, they had a value of $2,076,554,753 at the time of sale. Only a few nonferrous metal mining fields can top that record in either tons of output or value. In 1950 Bureau of Mines engineers estimated that the district still contains 66,100,000 tons of crude ore that would mill out to almost three million tons of zinc and lead concentrates. Much of this reserve is in Missouri because these fields were abandoned before being fully mined out. Unfortunately the ore is low-grade and is not profitable to mine at prevailing prices, but it is an important national reserve that some day may be utilized.

The collapse of mining dealt Joplin's economy a severe blow and led area leaders to undertake a concerted drive to attract new industry. Fortunately the mining era had given Joplin a considerable industrial base on which to build as well as making it the transportation and retail trade hub of the district.

The Korean War, which began on June 27, 1950, did not have the impact on Joplin that other wars had, although it did help civic leaders bring in new industry. The war inspired no large scale patriotic rallies or parades, though eventually seventeen of Joplin's young men died in the conflict.

The city gained its first important new industry in June 1951 when Vickers, Inc. announced plans to build a plant in Joplin. Vickers built their factory at Seventh and Schifferdecker Avenue and employed over 500 people in building precision hydraulic pumps and controls for military aircraft. The company later produced similar equipment for civilian use.

Another defense-related firm, the Pacific-Mercury Company, completed a plant in 1956 for the manufacture of electrical cables for the Boeing B-52 bomber. Employing as many as 550 at its peak in 1957, Pacific-Mercury sold its operation to Fairchild Cam-era and Instrument Company, a manufacturer of photo supplies and printing equipment. Later the cable manufacturing division of Fairchild came under the control of LaBarge Electronics while the printing equipment division passed to Solna, Inc.

A boom in housing construction was another significant factor in sustaining Joplin's economy as mining declined. In the first five years after World War II more than 1,000 new homes were built in the city. The availability of low interest rate loans and Federal Housing Authority and Veterans Administration guaranteed mortgages stimulated the boom. Most of the building centered in southeast Joplin where extensive new housing developments opened up.

Crime continued to be a problem as Joplin declined as a mining center, and no episode dramatized this more than the string of murders committed by William E. "Billy" Cook in early 1951. Cook, who had grown up amid the mine tailing piles of West Joplin during the Depression, brutally murdered an Illinois family of five and dumped their bodies in an abandoned mine shaft near West Fourth Street. He was later executed in California for another murder. The Cook episode generated much unfavorable national publicity for Joplin. The murder seemed symbolic of the social problems generated by the dying mining industry.

Joplin in the 1950s grew significantly as a cultural and entertainment center. In 1959 the Spiva Art Center opened in the Edward Zelleken house. Seven years later the Dorothea B. Hoover Historical Museum (now located next to the Tri-State Mineral Museum in Schifferdecker Park) was founded. Radio and television expanded rapidly after World War II. For twenty years the city had only one radio station, WMBH, but after World War II new licenses were issued and by 1980 five stations served Joplin. The city gained its first television station, KOAM-TV, in 1953, and KODE-TV and KSNF-TV were added in the next few years. The stations have played a significant part in expanding Joplin's role as a regional trade and cultural center.

The end of World War II brought a nationwide increase in the birthrate that soon put a strain on public schools. Joplin's R-8 school district responded with a program of expansion that made it one of the state's most respected public school systems.

In 1954, under longtime superintendent of schools, Roi S. Wood, the school district launched its most extensive building program. The largest project included five elementary schools and Parkwood High School.

Joplin schools became quite innovative in the post-World War II era. The Franklin Technical School offered an outstanding vocational arts program and occasionally undertook specialized

The "Ranger Ed" television show was produced locally in the late 1950s through the 1960s. Fon "Ed" Wilson hosted this children's variety show which featured film cartoons and guests. Courtesy, KODE-TV

Facing page, top left: Dr. H. Chris Oltman, Joplin's mayor from 1950 to 1954, was the last to hold that office under the commission form of government and the last mayor to be elected by a direct vote of the people. Under the new council-manager government, mayors are elected by the council from among their own members. Courtesy, Joplin Globe

Top right: Joplin's first woman mayor, Lena G. Beal, served two terms between 1972 and 1976. In 1968 she also became the first woman elected to the city council. Beal was the longtime president of the Joplin Business College and is active in civic affairs. Courtesy, Lena G. Beal

Bottom: Piles of gleaming white chat were still common in the Joplin area in the 1950s. Many of these tailing piles were reprocessed as advanced milling techniques made possible the recovery of minute ore particles. By the 1970s most of the piles had been hauled away for use as railroad ballast. From Massie—Missouri Resources Division. Courtesy, State Historical Society of Missouri

training programs for new industries locating in Joplin. The Joplin Reading Plan, initiated at Irving Elementary School in 1953, received national recognition and was widely copied. The high schools fielded a number of championship athletic teams, particularly under outstanding basketball and football coaches, Russ Kaminsky and Dewey Combs.

The 1950s ushered in a period when blacks made significant progress in Joplin. The crucial turning point came with the United States Supreme Court's decision of Brown v. Board of Education which held that segregated schools were unconstitutional. Immediate steps were taken to integrate the junior and senior high schools starting in 1955. Integration of the elementary schools followed in stages and was completed by the early 1960s. The city also began to integrate its black population more fully into the municipal work force and positions of public trust. M.W. Dial, principal of Lincoln School and longtime leader in the black community, was elected to the city council in 1954. Cozetta Thompson, a former administrator of the Joplin Business College, served three terms on the Joplin R-8 Board of Education in the 1960s and 1970s.

By the early 1950s many of Joplin's leaders called for changes in the municipal government to enable it to cope better with the readjustments necessitated by the end of the mining era. In 1914 Joplin had become the first city in Missouri to adopt the commission form of government. However, after forty years experience, many observers felt this type of government hampered effective action because the commissioners served as both administrators and policymakers. In early 1954 Joplinites voted to establish a council-manager type of government that would limit the nine-member council to policy-making functions while a hired city manager assumed overall responsibility for administering the city. In April 1954 the new government took over and the council elected Freeman R. Johnson as mayor and selected J.D. Baughman as the first city manager.

The 1960 census showed a count for Joplin of 38,958, a minute gain of 433 people over the 1950 figure. Though seemingly a disappointment, it indicated that the municipality had gained enough new business to offset the loss of mining-related jobs at a time when the Tri-State district as a whole lost population.

The 1960s saw Joplin continue the pattern of progress established in the prior decade as the city broadened its economic, cultural, and educational base. This diversification has been one of the chief hallmarks in Joplin's advancement since the end of the mining era.

A major factor in Joplin's future development was the estab-

Leon C. Billingsly, first president of Missouri Southern State College, played a leading role in shaping the college into an important four-year institution during his fourteen-year tenure. Billingsly became dean of Joplin Junior College in 1961 and three years later was appointed president of the newly organized Jasper County Junior College, which soon became Missouri Southern College. Courtesy, Missouri Southern State College

lishment of an interstate highway system. The new routes planned for this network assured that Interstate 44 would pass through Joplin's southern environs to replace the legendary Highway 66 that ran through the heart of the city. In 1955 Oklahoma began construction of a turnpike that ran from the state line to Tulsa. The Missouri State Highway Department then constructed a nine-mile extension from the state line to a point just south of Gateway Drive where it intersected with Highway 71 (Range Line). This formed the first segment of Interstate 44 in the Joplin area. Essentially complete through Missouri and Oklahoma by the late 1960s, this new traffic artery assured the continued growth of Joplin. It attracted new business and was a great stimulus to tourism and to the trucking industry. By 1965 some eighteen truck lines served Joplin, and Crown Coach and Greyhound had important bus terminals in the city.

Joplin continued to be served by five railroads giving the area excellent freight connections but rail passenger service, in keeping with a nationwide trend, declined steadily. In the early 1960s the Missouri Pacific and the Frisco dropped passenger service and on November 2, 1969, the Kansas City Southern's "Southern Belle" made the last railroad passenger run through Joplin.

With the decline of rail service, Joplin's municipal airport emerged as a major passenger terminal. Bond issues passed in 1955 and 1967 provided for lengthening the runways to accomodate large airliners. In 1965 the American, Central, and Ozark Airlines served Joplin.

Another major boost to Joplin's continued growth came with the establishment of Missouri Southern State College. Though Joplin Junior College had operated since 1937, district leaders thought the area needed a four-year institution. As a first step, voters approved establishment of an expanded Jasper County Junior College district in 1964. Fred Hughes became president of the new Board of Trustees and selected Dr. Leon C. Billingsly as first president of the college. In 1965 Senator Richard Webster and representatives Robert Ellis Young and Robert Warden played a leading role in securing the Missouri General Assembly's passage of a bill that provided for a four-year institution with state funding of the upper two years. The college moved to its new Mission Hills campus, built with a $2,500,000 bond issue, on June 7, 1967. Greatly expanded over the years, the college became a fully state-funded institution in 1977. Enrollment by the early 1980s averaged about 4,100. As forseen by its original promoters, the college has been of inestimable value in providing expanded educational opportunities and in creating a climate favorable to economic growth and cultural development of the district.

Another important institution of higher learning is the Ozark Bible College. This school moved to Joplin in 1944 from Harrison, Arkansas. Its new campus encompasses 110 acres and student enrollment averages more than 800. Dedicated to training men and women for Christian service, the college has long emphasized the field of music ministry and operates its own radio station, KOBC.

Joplin has produced a number of important figures in the entertainment industry. The most prominent of these in the post-World War II period have been Bob Cummings, Dennis Weaver, and John Beal. All three grew up in Joplin and gained prominence as actors on Broadway, in movies, and on television. Cummings and Weaver, in particular, have participated in a number of activities in their hometown.

Federal subsidy programs have been important to Joplin's welfare since the Depression. Among the most significant of these in the post-World War II period have been urban renewal projects which utilized federal grants to clear and rehabilitate deteriorating neighborhoods.

Actual work began in the 1950s with the Prehm project in southwest Joplin followed by the Parr Hill project in southeast Joplin in an area lying south of Fifteenth Street and east of the Kansas City Southern Railroad tracks.

The most controversial of the urban renewal programs were two downtown projects. The first of these, termed Progress, involved clearing thirty-five acres in the northeast part of downtown in which such historic structures as the Worth building succumbed to the wrecker's ball. This clearance made way for a number of new developments including Spiva Park, the Pentacostal Church headquarters, Messenger Towers, and the new Municipal Building.

Widespread opposition began to develop nationwide to these "federal bulldozer" programs that involved the razing of old neighborhoods. Locally the *Times-Observer* and the Good Government League mounted a publicity campaign that led to a 1970 referendum in which the electorate voted to discontinue Joplin's land clearance projects. The state attorney general, however, ruled that the city could not legally abandon the programs.

Faced with this growing opposition, officials modified the final program, the Downtown Urban Renewal project, to emphasize rehabilitation of existing structures and the creation of a modified mall between Fourth and Eighth on Main Street. The modified plan called for new sidewalks and shrubbery, and removal of parking, but retention of through traffic. Original plans had been to turn this section of Main into a pedestrian mall.

Above: Screen and television actor Dennis Weaver and his wife, Gerry, are shown here with Joplin Little Theatre board members in October 1967 when Weaver was awarded an honorary lifetime membership in the theatre. Born in 1925, Weaver was raised in Joplin and attended Joplin Junior College. While a student at the University of Oklahoma, he led his track and field team to the national championships. Courtesy, Jo Raudenbush

Facing page, top left: The Keystone Hotel, located at Fourth and Main streets, succumbed to urban renewal during the second phase of the downtown renovation program. In this 1969 photo the spires have already been removed from atop their turrets as demolition gets underway. The hotel was constructed in 1892; the top floor and the annex were added in 1899. Courtesy, Dorothea B. Hoover Historical Museum

Top right: This structure on Main Street is a good example of the efforts being made to preserve historic buildings in the downtown district. Constructed in 1877, the building has been completely renovated; the lower floor now houses a business and the upper story has been converted into a spacious townhouse featuring fixtures from the Connor Hotel. Courtesy, Louis Kanakis

Bottom: The Worth building at Fourth and Main streets was razed as part of the Progress urban renewal project soon after this photo was taken. The beauty of its architecture suggests why these land clearance projects were so controversial. Spiva Park now occupies this site. Courtesy, Rolla Stephens Realty

The greatest controversy involving historic buildings arose over razing the Connor Hotel, but this did not involve the original urban renewal programs. The Connor became an economic liability as travelers sought accommodations close to the main traffic routes and in 1969 it was closed as a hotel. Ownership passed to a local realtor who listed the structure on the National Register of Historic places in an effort to obtain federal grants and local backing for renovating the building. This effort failed and the realtor signed an option to sell the structure so that it could be torn down and a new public library built on the site. Local groups fought removal of the hotel from the National Register of Historic places and sought to work out a plan by which the grand old structure could be saved. All these efforts failed and the Connor was slated for destruction on November 12, 1978, but collapsed the day before as workmen prepared it for demolition. Three workmen were trapped in the debris and Joplin became the focus of nationwide attention while rescuers toiled around the clock to uncover the men. One of the workmen, Alfred Summers, was injured but alive after being trapped eighty-two hours in a void formed by the debris. Later, the other men, Thomas Oakes and Frederick Coe, were found crushed to death under the rubble.

One area of major growth in Joplin since World War II has been the medical profession. Oak Hill Osteopathic Hospital moved to a new facility on East Thirty-fourth Street in 1963. During 1967 the Joplin Regional Diagnostic Clinic, a state institution for treatment of the mentally retarded, opened on Newman Road. The next year St. John's Hospital moved to a new facility. Renamed St. John's Regional Medical Center and greatly expanded, it is now one of southwest Missouri's most extensive medical complexes. In 1975 Freeman Hospital moved to a new building on West Thirty-second Street.

A major shift in its tax base in the late 1960s enabled the Joplin municipal government to become much more progressive. In 1969 voters approved a new one-cent sales tax to shift a substantial part of the revenue burden from Joplin's property owners to non-residents who shopped in the city's extensive retail outlets. The increased revenues enabled the city administration to launch an expanded program of street improvements and improved social services. In 1983 voters approved an additional one-half of one percent transportation sales tax to bring about a further realignment in the revenue base.

Joplin made important progress in the 1960s and no decade has surpassed it in the broad diversification of the city's economic base. The 1970 census showed Joplin at a population of 39,256, an

This photo was taken about thirty minutes after the Connor Hotel collapsed on November 11, 1978. Spectators and workmen are beginning to arrive as the long task of searching for three trapped workmen begins. One of the three miraculously survived. Apparently weakened by the workers' cutting torches as they prepared the structure for demolition, one eyewitness reported the Connor swayed "like a serpent" before collapsing. Photo by G.K. Renner.

This view of the Westside Trailer Court on West Seventh Street shows the wreckage of mobile homes left in the wake of the May 11, 1973, tornadic cyclone. Two people died at this site while another fatality occurred in southeast Joplin. The seventy to one hundred mile-per-hour winds caused widespread damage across the city and dumped about two inches of marble-sized hail on the ground. Damage was particularly heavy in the Range Line area. Photo by Baird Studios. Courtesy, Joplin Globe

increase of only 298 people over the previous decade, but the figure was misleading because adjacent suburban areas had shown substantial growth.

One of the most spectacular developments in Joplin since World War II has been the growth of the Range Line business district. The construction of Interstate 44, which intersected with Range Line (U.S. 71) south of the city, and the rebuilding of the latter into a major four-lane thoroughfare in the late 1950s set the stage for its growth.

The thoroughfare soon began to blossom with numerous motels, restaurants, shopping centers, and other businesses. The first major motel on South Range Line was Mickey Mantle's Holiday Inn which opened in 1957 with a ceremony attended by many of Mantle's New York Yankee teammates.

A counterpart of the Range Line development and the growth of new shopping malls has been the decline of Joplin's downtown retail district. Main Street between First and Eighth had been the city's dominant shopping center since the 1870s, but an exodus began with the completion of Eastmoreland Plaza in 1956. This sixteen-acre center, located on East Seventh Street, was Joplin's first suburban shopping center. Other neighborhood centers soon followed on West Seventh, Twentieth, and Thirty-second streets. The most significant development was the completion of Northpark Mall on Range Line in 1972.

The collapse of Joplin's public transit system also accelerated the downtown district's decline. Evening and Sunday bus service terminated as early as 1952 and all municipal transit service ended in 1970. This left Joplin with taxicab service within the city and intercity lines that served municipalities on the main highways. By the 1980s, however, OATS, Inc. was providing transit for the elderly and handicapped on an informal schedule basis.

The controversial Vietnam War did not cause the unrest in Joplin that it did in some parts of the country. The long war period was one of general prosperity and unemployment reached a record low of 3.3 percent in 1972. Some twenty-three of Joplin's young men died in the conflict.

Joplin's experience disproved the old adage that tornadoes never strike twice in the same place when devastating storms struck in 1971 and in 1973 with a minor twister in 1972. The first tornado struck at dusk on May 5, 1971. Cutting a swath several blocks wide as it moved northeast across the city, the storm killed one person, injured at least sixty, and did approximately seven million dollars damage. The deadly storm that struck at dawn on May 11, 1973, killed three and injured more than 100. Termed a tornadic cyclone, the hurricane-like winds damaged buildings throughout the city and uprooted more than 1,000 trees. Damage amounted to $12,800,000 and President Nixon proclaimed Jasper and New-ton counties disaster areas.

Three years after the last tornado, Joplin suffered one of its worst floods in memory. Nearly eight inches of rain fell down-town in the twenty-four hour period ending July 3, 1976. Willow Branch, which flows under Main Street, inundated the downtown shopping center as it has a number of times in the past. Flood waters along Joplin and Turkey creeks also caused damage.

In 1973 Joplin celebrated its centennial. The festivities ex-tended from June 24 to July 4 and ended with an "Old-Fashioned Fourth" celebration. The highlight was the unveiling of Thomas Hart Benton's mural, "Joplin at the Turn of the Century, 1896-1906." Governor Christopher Bond and Benton spoke at the cer-emony and President Richard Nixon sent his best wishes.

The census of 1980 showed the Joplin city limits with a pop-ulation of 39,023, slightly below the 1970 total. City promoters were disappointed with the decline, the first in sixty years, be-cause they were conscious of the great strides Joplin had made, but they realized the loss reflected a general shift to the suburbs that was nationwide. In reality the Joplin area had experienced a healthy rate of growth. Almost unnoticed, the villages and towns surrounding Joplin had begun to grow faster than the city, partic-ularly after 1960. The 1980 census showed fourteen villages with a combined population of 5,195 adjoining the city's boundaries. In addition, the important towns of Carl Junction, Carterville, and Webb City, immediately to the north of Joplin, grew by an im-pressive 28 percent during the 1970s and Jasper and Newton counties showed a significant 13 percent increase.

In the wake of the 1980 count, the census bureau proclaimed Joplin a "Standard Metropolitan Statistical Area" (SMSA). The designation not only added to Joplin's status but also made it eli-gible for additional federal community development block grant monies and other benefits.

As Joplin moved into the 1980s industry continued to expand, with trucking showing the most spectacular growth. This industry began to burgeon in the 1960s and 1970s with the completion of Interstate 44, the relaxing of government regulations, and the re-placement of unionized drivers with owner-operators. This sys-tem, under which the drivers own their truck-tractors but pull company-owned semi-trailers, fits in well with the Four-State dis-trict's independent-minded work force. It is reminiscent of the early days of mining when hundreds of small operators worked their own small leases.

The electronics industry has also moved to the forefront

Nationally known artist Thomas Hart Benton was born in Neosho in 1889. He studied art in Chicago and Paris and later taught at Bryn Mawr, Dartmouth, and the Art Students League of New York. In the 1930s his style, termed regionalism, was hailed as a truly American style of painting and he received the Gold Medal Award of the Architectural League of New York. Benton is seen here working on his last project—a mural for the Country Western Hall of Fame. Photo by Bob Barrett

among Joplin employers and holds great promise for the future. Joplin's four principal electronics plants, Eagle-Picher Industries, Inc., Motorola, Inc., Midcon Cables, Inc., and LaBarge, Inc., employ more than 1,700 people.

Joplin's municipal government and the chamber of commerce continued their efforts to recruit new industry for Joplin. In 1979 the city council created the Joplin Industrial Development Authority with the power to issue industrial revenue bonds that give new industries or expanding ones special tax concessions. The Authority also established a 100-acre industrial park on North Range Line to provide sites for new industry.

Some thirty years have now passed since the closing of the mines and the bustling days of the past are only a legend to a younger generation. Today Joplin is a quieter city and the rowdy, crime-ridden image of an earlier time—always somewhat unfair—has disappeared.

Joplin has become, among other things, an attractive retirement center. Blessed with one of the nation's lowest cost-of-living scales, extensive medical facilities, good transportation, a splendid shopping establishment, and comfortable housing, the municipality has much to offer elderly people. Approximately 25 percent of Joplin's population receives social security benefits. This tends to make the average income level appear low in statistics and means that the area has a small work force relative to its overall population.

Joplin has successfully weathered the crisis brought on by the demise of mining and its economy is now broad-based and stable. Despite the collapse of mining, the city has experienced a steady rate of growth in the last sixty years. The natural bonanza that gave birth to the city in the first place is not likely to be duplicated. But Joplin's position as the regional center of the Four-State district appears to be secure because of the municipality's extensive retail and service facilities, its excellent transportation connections, its stable, industrious work force and magnificent medical services which are likely to stimulate further growth. So Joplin looks forward with confidence to further prosperity.

Picnicking at Reding's Mill, located south of Joplin on Shoal Creek, was very popular for many years. This oil painting, by Darral Dishman, captures the peacefulness of a family outing on a warm autumn Sunday in the early 1900s. The mill was destroyed by fire in 1932 but the foundation of natural rock still remains. Dishman was a talented artist whose works are prized by Tri-State area collectors. He taught art at Missouri Southern State College from 1966 until his death in 1984. From the artist's collection

Left: Mine Hopper *depicts the ubiquitous structures that stood over the mine shaft openings and housed the hoisting machinery. In many ways they were the nerve centers of the mines and sometimes were enclosed to provide more protection from the elements. Painting by Darral Dishman. Courtesy, First National Mercantile Bank*

Below: This watercolor portrays the mule barn at Sixth and Grey on a cold winter day in the early 1900s. Mules pulled heavy ore cars in the mines and wagons in the city. Painting by Darral Dishman. Courtesy, Mr. and Mrs. Ray Sharp

This watercolor of Joplin's Union Depot
suggests the hustle and excitement when a
train arrived. It captures the mood of the
1940s at the height of the passenger train age.
The station, designed by Louis Curtiss, was
placed on the National Register of Historic
Places in 1972. Painting by Darral Dishman.
Courtesy, Mr. and Mrs. Ray Sharp

Facing page, top: This watercolor shows "Holly Hill," also known as the Elias E. Pinkard home. Located on Duquesne Road, it was built by Robert Jameson in 1847/1848 on the site of the Great Western Spring, a favorite stopping place for pioneers traveling along the Turkey Creek road. Jameson reportedly was killed in the living room by Civil War bushwackers and buried in the yard under a cedar tree by his widow. Painting by Darral Dishman. From the artist's collection

Bottom: The Rothanbarger residence (also known as History House) is the oldest home in Joplin. Located on the north bank of Turkey Creek at Florida Avenue, Rothanbarger constructed the edifice with his own hand-pressed bricks and had partially completed it by the Civil War when bushwackers set it afire. They succeeded only in charring the rafters in the kitchen. Painting by Darral Dishman. Courtesy, Myral Butler

Right: In this watercolor, titled Fixing a Head Lamp, *a miner pauses to check his carbide light before riding an ore bucket into the murky depths of the mine. Painting by Darral Dishman. Courtesy, Mr. and Mrs. Ray Sharp*

Top: The new Joplin Municipal Building, completed in 1967, was built with the support of a $1,300,000 bond issue and replaced the dilapidated city hall which dated back to 1906. The new structure houses city offices, the fire and police departments, and the civil defense headquarters. Photo by G.K. Renner.

Above: Grand Falls, located on Shoal Creek in southwest Joplin, has always been the city's most spectacular scenic wonder. Photo by G.K. Renner.

Facing page, top: Colorful umbrellas brighten the scene as 1984 Homecoming Day celebrants attend a football game between Missouri Southern State College and Kearney State College in an October rain. Courtesy, Missouri Southern State College

Bottom: In this May 1983 scene Missouri Southern State College seniors are proceeding to commencement exercises. The faculty customarily lead the procession to Hughes Stadium for the ceremonies, but in this instance the threat of rain caused the program to be held in Taylor Auditorium. Courtesy, Missouri Southern State College

CHAPTER SEVEN

Partners In Progress

This statue of a miner is in Spiva Park at the northeast corner of Fourth and Main streets. Made of Italian marble and located in the heart of the downtown business district, the statue symbolizes Joplin's mining past. The park and the statue were given to the city in 1966 by George A. Spiva in memory of his father. Photo by G.K. Renner.

The historical continuity of business is largely brought about by the steady growth and development of a city. Joplin's growth and development has not been steady because it was a city founded and almost entirely supported by the unique industry of mining.

Because its products are internationally distributed, mining has always had an irregular boom-and-bust development. More important for Joplin was that mining, which started at the time of the city's incorporation in the 1870s, produced more than 25 percent of the Free World's zinc output in the 1940s, had almost no effect in the 1960s, and vanished completely in the mid-1970s.

As a result, Joplin's businesses, many of which were tied to mining, necessarily vanished or changed completely. Many cities in the West and in the Midwest that were linked to mining became ghosts, but not so Joplin.

Joplin, established at an important road junction, bounded on the north by fertile farmland and on the south by beautiful, natural, and unspoiled wild land, was blessed by a brightly varied and pleasant climate. As a result, it became the center of a wide, attractive area in which to live and enjoy life. The city transformed its mining industries into diversified services for happy living, and its mining heritage of individual effort and joy of life into productive contributions for the good of the whole area.

The organizations whose stories are detailed on the following pages have chosen to support this important literary and civic project. They illustrate the variety of ways in which individuals and their businesses have contributed to the city's growth and development. The civic involvement of Joplin's businesses, institutions of learning, and local government, in cooperation with its citizens, has made the community an excellent place to live and work.

JOPLIN HISTORICAL SOCIETY

The Joplin Historical Society was founded on June 17, 1966, due to the efforts of Dorothea B. Hoover, a member of an old Joplin mercantile family, the Bliedungs. She had collected historical material for many years, and was the organization's first president. Its business clearly stated was: "Bring together those interested in the history of the Joplin historical area. Understanding the history of our community is basic to our democratic way of life, gives us a better understanding of our city, state, and nation, and promotes a better appreciation of our American heritage."

The society's membership soon exceeded 600, and it embarked on several projects, all of which are still pursued. Data was compiled on the history of Joplin. The Tri-State Mineral Museum assisted. Plans for a future historical museum were made. Genealogical data was researched.

In 1973 the society sponsored the Centennial of Joplin, and as part of the celebration started the Dorothea B. Hoover Historical Museum. The name honored the organization's founder, who died in 1972. A guild to run the museum was started, largely due to the efforts of Dr. Winfred and Elizabeth Post, who had, like Dorothea, accumulated much valuable historical, as well as artistic, material. In 1976 the museum moved to a new site by the side of the Tri-State Mineral Museum in Schifferdecker Park. This became the headquarters of the Joplin Historical Society.

In 1981 the society and the guild merged and now operate the museum, with generous assistance from the Joplin city government. It embarked on a thoroughly efficient and

Dorothea B. Hoover, founder of the Joplin Historical Society, received the Rex Plumbum Award from the organization in 1971.

up-to-date program of preservation, cataloging, and display of historical documents and pictures, making them available to all who are interested. In 1984 the society began to offer working scholarships to students of Missouri Southern State College to research local history. The students receive three hours' credit.

This book is an outcome of an important aim of the Joplin Historical Society: the dissemination of local history.

The Dorothea B. Hoover Historical Museum contains a Victorian room exhibit that features a half-tester bed. The bed was made in New Orleans during the 1880s and, after being shipped up the Mississippi River to St. Louis, was brought to Joplin by wagon.

ELECTRIC MOTOR SUPPLY, INC.

The return of the warrior is often the beginning of a new business. So it was that Melvin Macy, an Army officer coming back from World War II in 1946 to Webb City, Missouri, started Macy Electric, a service and repair business for small electric motors. In 1947 Macy took in another World War II veteran, William Pickett, as a partner. Macy and Pickett met in the Joplin National Guard Wing, which saw war service in Alaska, and they had found one another to be expert electricians.

In the fall of 1948 Macy decided that perhaps the dangers from the enemy were less worrisome than from competitors, and returned to the Army after selling his share of the business to Harry J. Allman. Pickett and Allman renamed the concern Electric Motor Supply.

The firm began with two employees—the owners, who worked without pay for the first month and then took a monthly salary of $300 each. The company continued providing repair services on small motors, but as it prospered it catered to a growing need for new replacement motors and related electrical equipment. The firm soon began rebuilding and selling a wide variety of electrical equipment in the four-state area of Missouri, Kansas, Oklahoma, and Arkansas.

On March 11, 1954, the company was incorporated as Electric Motor Supply, Inc., and was authorized to issue 300 shares of stock. One-half of the initial stock distribution was issued to William Pickett as president and one-half to Naomi Allman as vice-president and Harry Allman as secretary/treasurer. The next year the company moved to 215 Wall Avenue in Joplin.

Michael Pence, who worked for Franklin Electric Company of Bluffton, Indiana, was transferred to Tulsa, Oklahoma. There he met and married his wife, Andrea, who was from Independence, Kansas. Though Pence was soon transferred back to Indiana, he was impressed with the quality of life and the opportunities available in the Joplin area. He decided to look for a small business there that he might purchase. Franklin had connections with Electric Motor Supply, which brought it to Pence's attention, and on November 1, 1971, the Pences bought the company.

With Michael as president and Andrea as secretary/treasurer, the firm expanded aggressively. In nine years its business volume increased four times. In addition to electric motors, products handled grew to include air compressors, blowers, hoists, pumps, tools, transformers, and much more. To handle the greatly increased business, the company built a modern new facility at 2301 West Twentieth Street in 1980 with the help of Industrial Revenue Bonds from the Joplin Industrial Development Authority.

Michael Pence has been active in

The firm was originally located at 111 East Daugherty in Webb City. Pictured are founders William Pickett (left) and Harry J. Allman.

many community organizations, having served as president of the Joplin Rotary Club, the Joplin Chamber of Commerce, and Twin Hills Golf and Country Club. He was the founding president of Metro 2000, a grass roots movement for progress in the Jasper/Newton County metropolitan area.

Electric Motor Supply, Inc., is proud of its past and excited about its future opportunities to provide an increased level of service to the four-state area.

Michael Pence, president (left), and Andrea Pence, secretary/treasurer, of Electric Motor Supply, Inc.

NEWMAN'S

Joseph Newman's Pierce City, Missouri, store was established in 1871.

Newman's is celebrating 113 years of business in Joplin as well as four generations of management by the same family.

Joseph Newman immigrated to this country from Germany before the Civil War, and came to Harrisburg, Pennsylvania, where he opened a small clothing store. The economic slump after the Civil War made Newman move west; he came as an itinerant peddler with the original settlers to Pierce City, Missouri, which was then the end of the railroad. Two years later, in 1871, he built his first store and founded the Newman Mercantile Company to sell clothing, gentlemen's furnishings, boots, and shoes.

Newman was successful in his business, fruitful in his family of nine children, and respected and honored in his town. His son, Sol, branched out on his own and started a store in Monett in 1890, and another son, Albert, and son-in-law Gabe Newburger opened a shop in Joplin in 1898.

Newman's in Joplin was located in the Wallower Building, erected in 1894 on the southeast corner of Main and Fourth streets, which later

Newman's department store at Sixth and Main streets in Joplin, circa 1910.

became the Keystone Hotel. The venture prospered, providing much needed elegance and fashion for both men and women in the rip-roaring mining town, and moved to a larger facility at 517 Main Street, which later became the site of Woolworth's. Sol Newman closed his Monett Store in 1907 and joined Newman's in Joplin.

In 1910 the Newmans erected a magnificent five-story building on the southwest corner of Main and Sixth streets. It cost $150,000 and was described by the *Joplin News Herald* of November 11, 1910, as "the model department store of the wide world." Perhaps it was. The article went on to tell its readers, "What they encountered as they passed the threshold after gazing at the immense show windows, floored in parquetry, wainscoted in mahogany, and mirrored and panelled in old ivory was a palatial home of merchandising."

The fixtures cost $91,300; the elevators, of solid bronze and tiled in rubber, cost $11,500. Other fixtures were of solid brass. The drinking fountain at the elevator entrance had solid bronze drinking cups and a marble basin; today it is just outside the entrance to the Dorothea B.

Hoover Historical Museum in Schifferdecker Park. The outside of the new building was remarkable, with its copper pediment, which is still extant, iron balconies, and copper sidewalk shades. Whereas the 1898 store employed about twelve people, the 1910 establishment employed more than 150 and rewarded them with an average wage of five dollars per week, which was a fair standard for the time.

About 1917 the store was further embellished by an unknown itinerant who made a remarkable series of stained-glass screens for the main lobby. A fine relic of these now underlies the boardroom table of the Newman Mercantile Company at Northpark Mall. The establishment also erected what was probably the largest illuminated sign in Joplin, on the top of the new building, and several pictures show that the staff was in the habit of having company picnics on the roof in its shadow.

In 1922 the firm expanded by purchasing the Kennedy Dry Goods Company in Enid, Oklahoma, and Joseph's son, Milton, managed that store until his death in 1943, at which time Joseph's grandson, Sol Jr., took over. Sol later moved to Joplin and became president of the firm until 1964, when he retired to Alabama. During this period and into the 1970s, Mark Ettinger, Joseph's grandson, was active in the management of the company.

In 1928 the firm expanded again, purchasing the Denneky Dry Goods Company in Cedar Rapids, Iowa, which was run by Gabe Newburger and his son, Buck, until the store closed in 1960. That same year Newman's entered the furniture business in Joplin at 732 Main Street and operated there until 1982.

Newman Mercantile Company, however, continued to expand and at present, besides the Joplin and Enid stores, operates stores in Springfield, Missouri; Pittsburg, Kansas; and

The ladies' ready-to-wear department, which was located on the third floor, circa 1910.

Midwest City, Oklahoma; and by 1985 will open a store in Hutchinson, Kansas.

A giant step was made on August 5, 1972, by William S. Schwab, Jr., when Newman's left its old building and moved into Northpark Mall on the east side of North Range Line in Joplin. Schwab is Joseph Newman's great-grandson, and he purchased the Newman Mercantile Company in 1966. Due in part to his efforts, the

Joseph Newman, founder of the Newman Mercantile Company.

first and largest covered mall in this part of the country was erected on North Range Line.

Newman's moved its store, lock, stock, and barrel, to the center of Northpark Mall. The construction of this mall, twenty-four blocks east of Main Street, and the relocation of Newman's and other well-known stores there, has radically altered the center of gravity of Joplin and its future growth. As the Greek philosopher Heraclitus said 2,500 years ago, "Nothing endures but change."

The Newman Mercantile Company continues its useful and prosperous course, with William S. Schwab, Jr., as chairman of the board and chief executive officer; J.R. Fortino as president; Robert E. Murray as vice-president/merchandising; and Rosemary Post as vice-president/marketing.

In contrast to the 1910 wages of five dollars per week, recently a saleswoman retired at more than $23,000 per year. Newman's has become a high-caliber clothing, accessories, and cosmetics store with a dedicated clientele, a community-oriented personnel, and a proud history.

COMMERCE BANK OF JOPLIN

The first year of the new century was coming to a close. Joplin was booming as zinc and lead were pouring out of its mines. The railroads had reached the city, and people were pouring in. Easterners in top hats were coming to Joplin to invest. World-famous entertainers played to overflowing and often tumultuous audiences.

It was during this time that C.M. DeGraff and some colleagues decided to found a new bank. The Citizen's State Bank was chartered on December 27, 1900, and was capitalized at $25,000. DeGraff became its first president, and 701 Main Street was its first location.

A charter subscriber was W.J.J. Leffen, who followed DeGraff as president in 1906, and whose son and grandsons have, with minor exceptions, been presidents and chairmen of the board up to today.

W.J.J. Leffen's father, William J. Leffen, was born in England about 1840 and later immigrated to America. He settled in Paola, Kansas, in the 1860s and started a flour mill. In 1872 he came to a still unincorporated Joplin.

What later was to be called Joplin had been platted as Murphysburg by Patrick Murphy. W.J.J. Leffen tied bags of fine lead ore on his insteps and practiced running so as to compete in foot races with Patrick Murphy, who was a champion runner.

Leffen bought a general store in the new boom mining town of Belleville, which has now disappeared, but was then north and west of Lone Elm Road. He borrowed $2,200 to do so and opened Wheeler and Leffen. The Belleville boom collapsed as the mines played out, but the business was moved to 510 Main Street and by 1900 had become a flourishing drugstore. At that time the Leffens became associated with DeGraff's new Citizen's State Bank. In 1903 the institution constructed a building at

W.J.J. Leffen, president, 1906-1941.

636 Main.

In 1906 W.J.J. Leffen became president of Citizen's State Bank and remained in that position for thirty-five years until his son, Stanford, succeeded him in 1941. Stanford was followed by his son, William F., in 1962, and he by his brother, John S., in 1968. John Leffen held the office until 1975 and was then named chairman.

In 1918 Stanford Leffen, who served as president for twenty-one years, volunteered in World War I as a U.S. Navy pilot. He learned to fly HS 2 and HS 12 seaplanes and still has the poster that inspired him to join hanging in his office at 624 Joplin Street. He was ready to leave from Pensacola, Florida, for France when Germany surrendered.

The Citizen's State Bank was small until World War II. In 1935 it still remained capitalized at $25,000 and had less than $.5 million in deposits. Yet it weathered the Great Depression when many small local banks did not.

World War II ushered in a boom for Joplin. The mines were pushed to

their limit to produce metal for the war effort. The construction in 1942 at Camp Crowder in Neosho, twenty miles away, brought 35,000 men to the area clamoring for a place to put their money. It was a banker's heyday.

The usual postwar depression did not materialize, and Citizen's State Bank prospered. In 1950 its name was shortened to Citizen's Bank. In 1955 the institution moved into better quarters at 701 Joplin Street and thereafter began branching out; in 1963 the Midtown Branch was opened at Fifteenth and Joplin streets.

A major step was taken in 1967, when the bank joined Commerce Bancshares of Kansas City and changed its name to Commerce Bank of Joplin. Commerce Bancshares is an affiliation of forty-four banks in Missouri, representing assets of more than four billion dollars, which was originally under the aegis of Commerce Bank of Kansas City. It is believed that this association allows small banks to compete successfully with larger ones, give enhanced service to their own communities, and thus, spur local growth as well as their own.

The main facility of the Commerce Bank of Joplin is located at Third and Main streets.

Results came soon. In response to increased business, on December 7, 1973, the Commerce Bank of Joplin moved again into the two lower floors of the newly built world head-quarters of the Pentecostal Church of God in America at Third and Main streets. The move was made over a weekend so that there would be no suspension of business. A good deal of engineering went into the moving and situating of heavy safes, deposit boxes, and storage units.

At the opening ceremony a string of fifty-dollar bills was cut—very carefully, as cutting currency is a federal offense. The bills were then donated to the United Fund of Joplin. Participating in this ceremony were John Leffen, bank president; Larry Hickey, president of the Joplin Chamber of Commerce; and Lena Beal, mayor of Joplin.

Two additional branch facilities were opened: the East Branch, at 1804 East Twentieth Street, in 1977,

Stanford Leffen, president, 1941-1962.

and the Southwest Branch, at 2980 McClelland Park Boulevard, in 1983. That same year the Midtown Branch was converted to an automated facility.

The expansion of Citizen's Bank into the Commerce Bank of Joplin occurred during crucial and occasion-

ally difficult times as the city was winding down from its position as the zinc-mining capital of the world. The slack was taken up by the growth of general industry, the en-hancement of natural resources, the development of retirement and voca-tional facilities, and the growth of its far-reaching medical facilities.

Commerce Bank, whose present capital of $5,253,000 compares favor-ably with the original capital of $25,000, and whose present assets exceed $70 million compared with less than $500,000 in assets in 1935, has been instrumental in much of Joplin's growth and will help to ensure its future.

The groundbreaking ceremonies for Com-merce Bank of Joplin, located at 2980 McClel-land Park Boulevard, took place in 1982. Be-hind is the old mining ground of Tanyard Hollow.

MCI TRANSPORTERS
Monkem Company, Inc.

Joplin was bound to become an important road transportation hub. It sits at the junction of the best transcontinental east-west road and a good north-south road linking the north center of the United States with the Gulf of Mexico and Texas. After World War II it appeared obvious that the highways were likely to inherit the earth.

In 1946 Ray Kempt and Arthur La Montagne formed a trucking company they called "Monkem," a combination of parts of both of their names. They had a contract with Tamko Asphalt Products Inc. of Joplin to carry their roofing shingles to markets in the Midwest. In 1947 Kempt bought out La Montagne, who moved to the East.

He incorporated the firm as Monkem Company, Inc., now known as MCI Transporters. The operation started with five tractor-trailer units and five drivers.

Monkem's original yard was located adjacent to Tamko's roofing plant at 601 High Street in Joplin, with offices also on Tamko's premises. In 1960 the firm moved to West Twentieth Street Road on the Missouri-Kansas state line.

On July 6, 1976, MCI Transporters was purchased by Lawrence "Larry" Kloeppel and his wife, Roberta "Bert." Prior to the purchase Larry and Bert were wheat farmers in Kingfisher, Oklahoma, Larry's birthplace. In 1957 they moved to Fort Scott, Kansas, where Larry was employed by Farmland Industries. In 1969 he joined the Midwestern Distributing Company, Inc., a trucking firm. Thus, by stages, Larry Kloeppel moved from "down on the farm" into the trucking industry.

Kloeppel became familiar with Monkem through his new position and discovered that the Kempts might agree to sell their firm. Their decision to buy the company was influenced by several factors. Joplin was the center of a good highway

Larry Kloeppel, president of MCI Transporters, and his wife, Bert, pose in front of one of their trucks.

system; they liked the area and the people in it; and they found in Joplin a nice friendly banker, the late Paul Buerge of First State Bank.

They purchased fifty acres north of Joplin to become the future home of MCI Transporters. On March 15, 1981, the Kloeppels moved into a newly constructed terminal on North Main Street Road in Joplin. It is a strikingly attractive terminal containing the corporate offices, and has the yards and buildings integrated into

the landscape.

The main office has a look evocative of the Southwest and is pleasantly decorated. The contrast between this and the older truck terminals is startling. MCI Transporters emphasizes the appearance of its trucks and its drivers, insisting that the units be clean and well maintained. MCI's drivers who, in essence are goodwill ambassadors and direct company representatives, are aware that their courteous attitude promotes the kind of image that encourages repeat business by shippers and receivers.

Monkem now covers the country from coast to coast, although 85 percent of its business is east of the Rockies, primarily in the central and eastern states. It now lives up to its charter and hauls all general commodities, except for moving households or explosives. MCI Transporters looks forward to increasing its moving units up to at least 750 and to the continuing expansion of its business.

An aerial of MCI Transporters, located on North Main Street Road.

HOWSMON'S OFFICE SUPPLY AND FURNITURE COMPANY

Hugh Howsmon.

Howsmon's Office Supply and Furniture Company began business as a bookstore on February 1, 1963, at 613 Main Street in Joplin.

At age twenty-six, Hugh Howsmon, who worked at Rocketdyne Company in Neosho, Missouri, and his wife, Lee Anne, who worked at Newman's in Joplin, had been married just one year. They had heard Spurgeon's Bookstore was for sale. The couple wanted a business of their own, but they had no experience in book sales. They owned a bookcase, a lamp, a cedar chest, and little else, yet they bought Spurgeon's, with the help of a grandmother and a friendly banker.

Spurgeon's Bookstore had a long history. It was originally Osterloh's Bookstore, founded in the 1890s, and had provided books and school stationery to Joplin students until 1950.

For the first two years Lee Anne ran the business and Hugh maintained his position at Rocketdyne. In 1965 the staff consisted of Hugh, Lee Anne, and one assistant, and they sold books, crafts, and hobby supplies. That year a complete stranger, Jack Adams, suggested that they sell office supplies. Crafts, which needed demonstration, did not give much return for the time spent. Book sales required patience and, if possible, an independent income.

Hugh was a great believer in a positive mental attitude. He had passed beyond *Think and Grow Rich* by Napoleon Hill. (Lee Anne had a copy rebound in real black leather to look like a Bible.) He had gone on to read *Success Through a Positive Mental Attitude* by Clement Stone and, inspired by this, jumped into the office supply business.

The Howsmons purchased a building at 610 Main Street in 1973, which had housed the old Coulter McGuire store. They moved office furniture into it and began phasing out books. Business grew, and the couple bought the old Ramsay Building on the northeast corner of Sixth and Main streets and moved all their supplies into three floors of the double-front facility.

They still needed more room so they bought structures at 527 and 529 Main Street. Just as things seemed to be going quite well the terrible 1976 flood deluged Main Street and the Howsmons had the misfortune of seeing $50,000 in uninsured merchandise floating in seven feet of water in their basements.

Despite the flood, business continued to grow, and in 1980 the couple purchased the five-story Christman Building, with 80,000 square feet of space, on the southeast corner of

Lee Anne Howsmon.

Fifth and Main streets. This structure was erected in 1917 for the Christman Dry Goods Company and was occupied by that firm until 1954, when Macy's took it over.

Retail sales were housed on the ground floor, and the other floors were packed with merchandise that was moved and stacked by sophisticated equipment, and overflowed into warehouses behind the buildings on Virginia Avenue. Much of this stock is distributed wholesale by the Howsmon Distributing Company over a wide area surrounding the city.

The Howsmons have moved from building to building along Main Street, and today, twenty-two years, nine facilities, two children, four trucks, and sixty-seven employees later, the couple continues to add new departments, such as art supplies and computer furniture and accessories, to their establishment.

The headquarters of Howsmon's Office Supply and Furniture Company is located at 501 Main Street in the old Christman Building. Photo by James Mueller, Joplin

OZARK MEMORIAL PARK CEMETERY

Ozark Memorial Park Cemetery was incorporated on February 2, 1928. The first president was F.H. Gager. George W. Crocker was one of the founding board members and was president from 1931 until his death in 1957.

Three generations of the Crocker family have operated Ozark Memorial Cemetery. George W. Crocker was followed by his son, George Eugene Crocker. His son, James E. Crocker, then took over as president after his father's death in 1968. A fourth generation is ready to enter the business; James has a son, Gregory Eugene, who is now a senior at Parkwood High School.

The site chosen for the cemetery was admirable, on heavily forested country in northeast Joplin. It was bounded by the old Schifferdecker estate on the north, Langston Hughes Broadway on the east and south, and St. Louis Avenue on the west. It is still surrounded by a heavy forest to the north and east. The north slopes down to Turkey Creek through the old Schifferdecker Gardens where people liked to relax in Joplin's early days.

The design was to retain the look of a garden. Markers were to be level with the ground with no upright tombstones. Floral decorations in permanent containers could be put out at any time.

The cemetery was to establish a perpetual care fund and according to Missouri regulations, 10 percent of all land sales must be put into an irrevocable trust fund for the maintenance of the cemetery. Ozark Memorial contributes at least 15 percent of its land sales to this fund, which is

An aerial view of Ozark Memorial Park Cemetery.

approaching $300,000.

After World War II public taste seemed to change. A plain, ungarnished landscape seemed less attractive than it once did, and the cemetery began designing gardens and adding sculptures and paintings.

In 1948 Ozark Memorial built the Garden of Memories, which contained a Bible with the Lord's Prayer carved on it, sculptured in granite, and the Garden of Gethsemane with a marble statue of Christ kneeling. In the 1950s the cemetery built the Garden of the Good Shepherd with the Twenty-third Psalm carved in granite on the feature. Also during that time a special section called Baby Land was set aside for infants up to eigh-

teen months of age, and in the 1970s another similar section, called Lullaby Land, was established. In 1979, in a new section, the Garden of Hope, was laid out with a marble sculpture of Jesus and his family.

In 1981 a 48-crypt above-ground mausoleum was built with sculptured praying hands above it. In 1984 a columbarium, a repository for cremation urns, was opened.

By 1985 Ozark Memorial Park Cemetery had received over 10,500 burials. Of interest to sports fans is the fact that Gabby Street, who came from Joplin and was a well-liked national sports announcer, was buried there in 1951.

Ozark Memorial Park Cemetery has added well over $100,000 worth of sculptures and art work and will continue to maintain and beautify its gardens. It is the cemetery's desire to provide a beautiful and comforting place where visitors can come to pay their respects.

The Garden of the Apostles, one of many gardens that are part of Ozark Memorial Park Cemetery.

JOPLIN BUILDING MATERIAL COMPANY

Joplin Building Material Company was founded in April 1963 by Dale Lundstrom and John R. Goostree. Their desire was to build a business based on quality, service, fairness, and friendliness. They were not quite sure what they were going to sell, so they decided the firm's name should encompass various types of materials.

The company's first office was at 602 East Fourth Street in a small Quonset hut beside the Kansas City Southern Railroad tracks in an area known as the Kansas City Bottoms. This was near the Joplin Branch, where a little farther downstream the lead that had started Joplin was discovered in 1869. The whole area was undermined.

The firm's first sales line was aluminum windows, storm sash, and garage doors. Soon it began specializing in brick and masonry products. The area where the bricks were stocked happened to be over an old mine drift, and on one occasion the owners and employees watched helplessly as 18,000 bricks disappeared into a hole in the ground. Seventy-five truckloads of fill were required to close the hole.

Initially, the company was run entirely by the founders. They prospered and tripled their business by 1966. Joplin Building Material was incorporated in 1965 and moved its office to the former Powell Truck Line building at the corner of Murphy Boulevard and Fifth Street. A ready-mix concrete plant was erected nearby.

In 1968 Lundstrom and Goostree purchased the old IGA warehouse at 1027 Main Street, moved their office there, and rented the rest of the 120,000-square-foot, five-story building under a new incorporation, the Joplin Warehouse Company.

In 1972 Joplin Building Material purchased the Concrete Masonry Products Company at the Joplin Stockyards. The next year Lundstrom and Goostree sold the Joplin Ware-

Dale Lundstrom (left) and John Goostree, founders.

house Company and returned their office to Murphy Boulevard and Fifth Street.

The business continued to expand, and in 1978 the pair purchased the Alexander Block and Building Material Company, located at 320 West Nineteenth Street in Baxter Springs, Kansas. Joplin Building Material began to concentrate on the making and sale of concrete blocks, with

which it has established and maintained a reputation for excellence. The blocks have been used in many construction projects in the Tri-State area, including hospitals, schools, malls, and fire stations.

John Goostree died in 1983, and Dale Lundstrom purchased his interest and became sole owner. That same year he sold the ready-mix plant and purchased the Joplin Burial Vault Company and began making several precast concrete products. Also in 1983 the Ozark Engineering Company headquarters at Fifteenth and Illinois Avenue was acquired and all operations of the Joplin Building Material Company were concentrated in one place, mechanized, and automated, with beneficial effects for both the company and its clients.

Since its beginning, the owners and staff of the Joplin Building Material Company have been active in civic and service projects with the Rotary, the Kiwanis, and the United Way Fund. The firm looks forward to a growing business locally and still maintains its emphasis on fairness and friendliness.

The Joplin Building Material Company is located at Fifteenth Street and Illinois Avenue.

FAG BEARINGS CORPORATION

To trace the history of FAG Bearings Corporation, one must go back quite a few decades, because that is when the idea that remains so important to the firm was originated—the idea of the "rolling motion and friction," which gave birth to FAG's antifriction bearings.

In Europe in 1817, a German by the name of Karl Drais created the "ordinary man's horse." The first bicycle, it had no pedals and was propelled by being shoved along by the rider's feet.

In 1852 another German, Philipp Moritz Fischer from Schweinfurt, Germany, added pedals to the "ordinary man's horse." With this innovation, something important had happened—man started to move by his own power, and he began to fully appreciate the energy-consuming effect of friction.

The FAG Bearings Corporation factory is located at 3900 Range Line.

The year 1883 is recognized as the beginning of the company known as FAG. In that year Friedrich Fischer, the son of Philipp Moritz, developed, experimented with, and eventually built a machine to manufacture steel balls using the "centerless principle," balls made in equal size, perfectly round, and evenly hardened. That process was patented in 1890 and remains, in principle, the way all balls for bearings are manufactured.

Georg Schaefer started another ball-bearing factory in his locksmith's premises in Schweinfurt, Germany, in 1885. In 1909, ten years after the death of Friedrich Fischer, Georg Schaefer acquired Fischer's factory and merged it with his own company. Since 1919 the company—FAG

Kugelfischer Georg Schaefer & Co.—has been under the exclusive personal responsibility of the Schaefer family. Accordingly, the name FAG means "Fischer Corporation."

After Georg Schaefer's death in 1925, his eldest son, Georg, who had joined the company in 1919, continued his father's work with energy and diligence. Despite the hardship brought about by the poor economic situation, the factory was modernized and new buildings were erected.

Since Schweinfurt was the center of the German roller bearing industry, it became the target for devastating air raids during World War II and its factories were reduced to ruins. It seemed the end of FAG Kugelfischer & Co. In 1948, after most of the rubble had been cleared away, production resumed under Dr. Schaefer's direction with the assistance of the United States and its allies. Exemplary new workshops were erected and equipped with the most modern machinery available to ensure top precision for the ball and roller bearings manufactured. The hot forging and rolling process of bearing rings was developed, and today FAG has one of the biggest and most modern ring-forging shops in the world.

The centerless grinder was invented by Friedrich Fischer of Schweinfurt, Germany, in 1883.

In 1954 FAG expanded abroad, establishing a branch plant in Stratford, Ontario, Canada. Instrumental in building this important manufacturing facility was Georg Schaefer, Jr. More branch plants followed in brisk succession in Brazil, India, Italy, Austria, Switzerland, Portugal, and Spain. The growth of the company is expressed by the fact that it now has various divisions and is represented in 135 countries. Today FAG manufactures the world's largest line of roller bearings, and other products such as hydraulic brake equipment, fuel injection pumps, grinding wheels, high-precision measuring instruments, and textile machinery accessories.

In January 1967, the Schaefer family made the decision to build a major bearing production facility in the United States. Otto Weth, in charge of the Stratford plant, was given the direction to select a site in the United States for this facility. The following June, Bob Leeming, sales manager of the Stratford plant, and Heinz Kleinhenz, in charge of quality control at Stratford, called on Gene White in Joplin, who was then president of Autotronics, Inc., a customer of FAG. During the course of the conversation, Leeming mentioned that they were looking for a site in the United States to construct a plant. White contacted Jada McGuire, manager of the Joplin Chamber of Commerce, who visited that same day with Leeming and Kleinhenz. The following year two groups from Joplin went to Canada to call on the FAG personnel in Stratford.

Under the direction of Otto Weth, 400 different cities in the United States were considered and a comprehensive study was made of ninety-five of these. In June 1968 Georg Schaefer, Jr., visited Joplin and met with Missouri Governor Warren E. Hearnes and a group of leading citizens, including Jerry Wells, assistant city attorney, Larry Hickey, president of the Joplin Chamber of Commerce, and Morgan Hillhouse, a local businessman, to confirm the selection of Joplin as the proposed site for FAG's future production facility. In July 1968 nine people from Joplin traveled to Schweinfurt, Germany, and at that time Georg Schaefer, Jr., advised that Joplin had been selected as the site for the firm's new production facility. He stated to those present that while many factors were involved in selecting Joplin, the primary reason was the optimistic and energetic attitude of the local people.

Later that year the citizens of Joplin approved the issuance of seven million dollars of industrial bonds by a 19-1 margin for the erection of the first building of the production facility.

Jerry Wells became the first president of FAG Bearings Corporation, and a site was chosen at 3900 Range Line overlooking the intersection of Interstate 44 and Highway 71. Construction was started in 1969 and Werner Ludwig, from the Stratford plant, arrived to supervise the undertaking. Ludwig established permanent residence in Joplin in 1970 and remains the operation's manager.

Construction was completed in 1970. The initial facility had one water pump bearing line and a total of thirty-five employees. A forge and another ball plant were added four years later, and in 1979 a heat-treating plant and other facilities were built.

The plant now has a complete forge shop, and the product lines include a wide range of spherical, deep groove, angular contact, cylindrical, and water pump bearings.

The selection of Joplin has proven to be an auspicious one. The number of employees has grown to 275, each working with sophisticated equipment in a model setting.

Participants in the opening ceremony for FAG Bearings Corporation's Joplin plant on June 8, 1970, were (from left to right) Mr. and Mrs. Otto T. Schaefer; Dr. and Mrs. Georg Schaefer; Warren Hearnes, governor of Missouri; and Georg Schaefer, Jr.

RUSSELL BELDEN ELECTRIC COMPANY

Russell Belden, founder. (1894-1951)

Charles Harmon Belden (1859-1945), a pioneer of the electrical industry, founded the Belden Electrical Supply Company, which was a precursor of the Russell Belden Electric Company, in 1899. Originally a printer, he learned the brand-new electrical business from a Professor Thompson whose firm evolved into the General Electric Company, in New Britain, Connecticut.

Belden came to Joplin in 1890 to install an electric street railway. His first office was at 220 West Fourth Street, but he soon moved to 412 Joplin Street, which was exciting because his back door opened onto the stage door of the old Club Theater.

Electricity was "lights" in those days, and the Belden Company wired the luxurious homes of the Bartlett, Murphy, Schifferdecker, Picher, and Zellican families. In 1906 it wired the 250 rooms of the Connor Hotel—for $1,400.

Electricity was beginning to be "power," however, encouraged by C.W. Hough, manager of the Consolidated Light and Power Company. Electric motors were occasionally used in the mines, and the firm installed many of them. The Beldens began to expand, completing electrical installations from Walla Walla, Washington, to Austin, Texas, and from Trinidad, Colorado, to Pensacola, Florida.

In 1914 Belden started the Chandelier Shop which retailed light fittings. Generally, however, the business evolved into electrical contracting. The World War I years were booming times for Joplin, the early 1920s were growth years for the whole country, and the electrical industry flourished. Mines and homes became completely electrified.

Russell Belden, one of Charles'

sons who worked as a salesman for the company, served overseas during World War I and rejoined the firm upon his return. In 1929 he formed his own business, the Russell Belden Electric Company, located at 313 West Thirteenth Street. Times were hard. The old Belden Company folded but Russell kept going.

World War II was a world catastrophe, but it provided work for Russell, who secured the contract to supply Camp Crowder at Neosho, Missouri, as well as several other wartime installations.

In 1947 Russell moved to 402½ Joplin Street, next door to where the Belden Company had started. The firm prospered and expanded to Fort Smith, Arkansas; Springfield, Missouri; and Hutchinson, Kansas.

Russell Belden died in 1951 and the company became a trust. Russell's son, Jack, took over in October 1961 and rebuilt the wide-ranging electrical business that Russell had enjoyed. Jack Belden became a city councilman and served from 1972 to 1984.

He also served as mayor from 1978 to 1982. The Russell Belden Electric Company, now located at 1027 Virginia Avenue, continues under his management to cover a wide range of electrical wholesaling.

Jack Belden, son of the founder, with sons Russ (left) and Scott, the third and fourth generations in the electrical business.

DUTCH VILLAGE MOTEL

The Dutch Village Motel was started by Joseph Mertz with eight units on West Seventh Street in 1955. At that time Robert Higgs, nationally known Joplin artist, was painting frescoes around town, and he painted a beautiful view of a Dutch village with a traditional windmill in the lobby of the new motel. It was from this picture that the facility obtained its name. This fresco was severely damaged by a fire in 1980 and has not been restored.

The motel expanded, and more units were added in 1958. About 1962 seventeen more units were built on the other side of the swimming pool, which was completed in 1965.

The motel has had several owners since 1967, including William and Virgil Owen and Pat Patterson. Don and Marlene McCowan purchased the motel in 1977 and continue to run it successfully.

Both of the owners came from Pretty Prairie, Kansas, fifty miles west of Wichita, a town with a population of about 500. Don's family came from County Down, Ireland, in the middle of the nineteenth century and settled, first in New York State, then in Ohio. Eventually, his great-grandfather homesteaded in Pretty Prairie during the 1870s. Marlene's family also homesteaded in Pretty Prairie about the same time as the McCowans.

Before taking over the motel, Don McCowan was a schoolteacher and then a salesman of educational material. In 1962 he went into driver's education, using simulators. Five years later he worked with the pharmaceutical division of Pfizer, Inc., and in 1972 graduated into hospital management. From there, it was an easy transition to managing a motel.

The McCowans like the personal nature of their work and feel that owner-operators of hostelries make guests feel wanted and contented. They have upgraded all the units and continue to do so.

Marlene McCowan, in front of a fresco painting of the Dutch Village by Robert Higgs.

In November 1980 the motel suffered a severe fire that was started by a motorist who ran into its gas meters. This unfortunate accident caused extensive damage to the front of the west wing of the motel, and partially destroyed Robert Higgs' large Dutch Village fresco.

Don McCowan has been very active in community affairs. From 1981 to 1984 he was president of the Joplin Hotel Motel Association. During this period a controversy raged over a city motel room tax, which the association opposed and the citizens of Joplin eventually voted down. McCowan believed that such a tax, if levied, should only be used for tourism. He is now a committee member of the Tourism Convention Board of Metro 2000, an organization dedicated to improving life in the Joplin area.

A swimming pool and comfortable rooms are just some of the amenities available at the Dutch Village Motel.

C.C. MACHINE, INC.

Some businesses are proud of being run by the same family for several generations, but C.C. Machine, Inc., is proud of being run by all members of the current generation. Its business is the rebuilding of automotive engines and the wholesaling and retailing of internal-combustion engine parts. The owners and managers are Mr. and Mrs. Clarence Clark; one of the bookkeepers is their daughter Kimberley Sue Ross; the secretary is daughter Cindy Rebecca McDade, who was a cam grinder; and their son, Kenny Clark, is a machinist and engine assembler. Kimberley, Cindy, and Kenny were all working in the business before they left high school.

Clarence Clark came from Stella, Missouri, and began working in Rogers, Arkansas, as a mechanic in 1962 in an auto engine rebuilding shop in which he eventually held part ownership. In 1964 he and his wife, Donnia, moved to Carthage, Missouri, and in the basement of 116 North Main Street started Clark's Machine, rebuilding auto engines.

Clark's move to Joplin was based on his assessment of a need for an auto rebuilding shop with modern precision equipment, especially auto crankshaft weld rebuilding and grinding machines. In 1965 he moved to 719 Pennsylvania Avenue.

The business started with limited equipment and has expanded to a staff of twenty-seven with highly sophisticated and partly automated cleaning, boring, welding, grinding, drilling, and testing machines worth more than $500,000.

The operation kept outgrowing its headquarters. In 1972 it moved to 1021 Moffet Avenue. This location proved too small in 1978 and the company moved again, to 1704 West Seventh Street. This building had been a shop where Vickers Inc. rebuilt hydraulic pumps. It measured 18,000 square feet in area. Plans are currently under way to expand this building by an additional 16,000

Clarence Clark and his wife, Donnia, are the owners of C.C. Machine, Inc.

square feet.

Originally, of course, Clark's Machine rebuilt any engine, including special models and classic car engines, and still performs some of this work. The business has evolved to handling fleets of cars, which is efficient because fewer models are involved.

In 1980 Clark was sitting in a cafe in Des Moines, Iowa, idly watching United Parcel Service (UPS) trucks go in and out of their terminal. This gave him an idea. He negotiated to rebuild some of their engines and ended up handling the rebuilding of UPS truck engines from at least ten central states between Colorado and Ohio.

Contrary to popular belief, Clark maintains that his rebuilt engines are more efficient than new engines. This is because his assembly is a hand operation. Parts are more closely matched than in mass production. The firm currently remakes 100 engines per month and shortly expects to increase that figure to 250. In 1983 Clark's Machine incorporated as C.C. Machine, Inc., with Clarence Clark as president and Donnia Clark as vice-president.

TAMKO ASPHALT PRODUCTS, INC.

At the beginning of 1985 Tamko Asphalt Products, Inc., consisted of approximately 1,100 employees at its six different manufacturing locations, and five selling warehouse locations. The manufacturing locations are at Joplin, Missouri (1944); Phillipsburg, Kansas (1969); Tuscaloosa, Alabama (1975); Knoxville, Tennessee (1977-paper mill); Frederick, Maryland (1979); and Dallas, Texas (1985).

At these locations and within these facilities are two glass mat manufacturing mills, four dry felt (paper) mills, four asphalt oxidizing units, and fourteen asphalt roofing mills.

The corporate officers of the company are Ethelmae Craig Humphreys, chairman of the board and secretary; J.P. Humphreys, president; Leland W. Browne, vice-president/operational analysis and management development; Leo J. Faneuf, vice-president/manufacturing; R.L. Allen, vice-president/sales; Odes L. Carder, vice-president/dry felt; and Lovern Ellis, treasurer and assistant secretary.

In May 1941 Lehrack Asphalt Roofs, Inc., was incorporated in Joplin by Otto J. Lehrack, Sr., Otto J. Lehrack, Jr. (both formerly of Kansas City, Missouri), and John Harold Cragin of Joplin. Their principal asset was the property at 601 North High Street in Joplin. Attempts were made to raise funds, and some very minimal activity was undertaken to start a building to house an asphalt roofing plant.

Later that year Otto Lehrack, Sr., died, and all activity came to a halt. Otto Lehrack, Jr., was disabled, and had never been involved in manufacturing asphalt roofing, so in March 1944 he sold the assets of Lehrack Asphalt Roofs, Inc., to E.L. Craig, Fred Wolfson, and Cheney Brewen—all formerly of Kansas City, Missouri. Shortly thereafter, at the suggestion of Mrs. E.L. Craig, the name of the company was changed to Tamko Asphalt Products, Inc., reflecting the states into which the

An aerial view of the firm's roofing plant in Frederick, Maryland.

company's product was intended to be sold—Texas, Arkansas, Missouri, Kansas, and Oklahoma.

E.L. Craig was the principal instigator and driving force behind Tamko. Production began in 1945. When the building of the roofing plant had been completed, Craig's first order was from the federal government for 90,000 rolls of chicken wire—three feet wide—to be enclosed on either side of the wire by saturated felt, a roofing product. The company's first price list was issued in January 1945.

Craig and Wolfson bought out the Brewen interest in 1947. And in late 1948 Wolfson's interest was also purchased by Craig. Shortly thereafter a portion of Tamko's stock was offered to each employee. And although most of that stock has been sold back to Tamko since then, a few employees remain stockholders.

E.L. Craig, his wife, Mary Ethel, and their daughter, Ethelmae, were the primary directors of the company until February 1960 when Craig died at the age of eighty-four. Upon her husband's death, Mary Ethel Craig

was named chairman of the board, J.P. Humphreys was named president, and Ethelmae Craig Humphreys was named vice-president and secretary. Mrs. Craig retired in 1972 and died in early 1984.

In the early years the firm was most fortunate to have employed such outstanding operating personnel as Odes Carder, felt mill manager; Karl Koos, roofing plant manager; Harry Kepke, maintenance supervisor; Curtis Staves, treasurer; as well as such stalwarts as Ray Baker, Cecil Evans, Rusty Haynes, Ben Holmes, "Little Pete" Pedersen, "Big Pete" Peterson, George Hosp, Buck Lundien, Bill Manz, Jr., Bob Page, Jack Richardson, Tom Ritter, Scott Plumb, Harold Downs, and Ralph Wilson.

Tamko Asphalt Products, Inc., has been blessed with unusually talented and unique employees. It is because of them that the company continues to grow.

ST. JOHN'S REGIONAL MEDICAL CENTER

Founded in Joplin by the Sisters of Mercy in a small frame structure in 1896, St. John's has grown from a ten-bed unit to a 367-bed regional medical center. The incentive to build the hospital started when Mother Mary Frances Sullivan and another Sister met a seriously injured miner near a Joplin railroad station who was being transferred on a stretcher to Fort Scott, Kansas, site of the nearest hospital. The nun feared that the man's condition would worsen greatly by the time he arrived in Fort Scott several hours later.

History records that the Sisters were deeply moved at the sight of the suffering miner. Mother Mary Frances Sullivan "laid the matter before her Sisters to see about the immediate opening of a small hospital." After obtaining their approval, she called a meeting of several Joplin businessmen to ask their help in establishing the hospital.

With the promise of hearty cooperation from the men who were in attendance, the Sisters set about furnishing a small frame house near

Mother Catherine McAuley (1778-1841), foundress of the Sisters of Mercy Order.

Tenth and Virginia, which a Gilbert Barbee placed at their disposal—rent free.

Calling it "Mercy Hospital," Mother Mary Frances and two other Sisters continued the work of their foundress, Catherine McAuley, in

caring for the sick and injured. Mother McAuley, an Irish heiress, used her inheritance to help those in need, provide shelter to homeless women, visit those that were sick and imprisoned, and educate the children of Dublin. With this philosophy, the Sisters of Mercy expanded their works to the United States, founding many schools and hospitals, such as Mercy Hospital in Joplin.

The little hospital was not long in outgrowing its ten-bed capacity. As a time-worn history found in St. John's archives continues, "The efficiency of the Sisters and their kindliness had so won for them the esteem and confidence of the public that a new and larger hospital was practically assured.

"By 1898," the record shows, "the mines were producing well, the city was spreading out toward the west and south, and comfortable homes, some large and more small, were springing up along the streets around and even far beyond the convent. Talk of the proposed permanent hospital building aroused interest among the townspeople, in whom new civic pride was stirring."

The Sisters and Joplin citizens raised money over a wide area locally, and their combined efforts founded St. John's Hospital on a site at Twenty-second and Connor Avenue that was given to them by Patrick Murphy, one of Joplin's founding fathers.

By 1898 the Sisters of Mercy had a fifty-room facility built of fine Carthage stone, called St. John's Hospital, named after St. John of God who was born in Portugal in 1495. After a roistering life as a courtier and soldier, John dedicated himself to serving the poor and suffering for God. He founded a hospital in Granada, Spain, and a religious order to carry on his work. The present St. John's

The original St. John's Hospital, founded by the Sisters of Mercy at Twenty-second Street and Connor Avenue. Photo circa 1900

Regional Medical Center has a statue commemorating him and depicting his great virtue of charity.

By 1903 St. John's Hospital School of Nursing was founded and Catherine Sullivan, R.N., from Manchester, New Hampshire, managed it. It was accredited in 1905, and five years later Sister Mary Alphonsus Brady took over and became the symbol of St. John's for several generations of Joplinites.

Disaster struck on August 4, 1914, at Tipton Ford, twelve miles south of Joplin. A Kansas City Southern train crashed, killing fifty-six people. The injured were all cared for at St. John's. In 1917-1919 the worldwide influenza epidemic hit. St. John's, understaffed due to the war and much undersized, managed with volunteer help from the women of Joplin.

The Joplin Globe reported with pride how St. John's nurses and Sisters responded to the Columbus, Kansas, tornado of 1937 in which twelve people were killed and 175 were injured. They drove to the scene in a blinding cloudburst and worked around the clock for the next few days at the site.

Joint efforts by the Sisters and the citizens of Joplin kept St. John's in the forefront of medical care and enlarged its facility in 1927, 1948, and again in 1958, when it was brought up to 190 beds, with all the necessary ancillary services. Nevertheless, projections showed the existing facilities were inadequate and the existing site incapable of the needed expansion.

The tremendous program to launch St. John's Regional Medical Center began by breaking ground at 2727 McClelland Boulevard in 1965. Three years later a new 267-bed center was occupied. In 1971 a 100-bed nursing building was added with new facilities in both therapy and outpatient services. Four years later this was changed to a rehabilitation center and named Brady Rehabilitation Building, in memory of Sister Mary

Alphonsus Brady who had served so well.

Expansion continued apace. A new Professional Building was constructed in 1978, the new Cardiovascular Unit in 1981, and the new, $30-million, nine-story tower in 1984.

Today St. John's offers a wide range of highly specialized diagnostic and therapeutic services. Serving a population area of 350,000 in the four-state area, people came to St. John's for medical expertise found in the Cardiovascular Center, Neurology Unit, Parkinson's Disease Treatment Center, Oncology Center, as well as other specialized programs.

Mercy Hospital, at Tenth Street and Virginia Avenue, was the first Sisters of Mercy-sponsored hospital. Photo circa 1896

With the largest number of private rooms in the area, its up-to-date facilities, and its commitment to following the ideals of the Sisters of Mercy, St. John's Regional Medical Center is a proud memorial to Sister Catherine McAuley, her fellow Sisters, and the citizens of Joplin.

St. John's Regional Medical Center, 2727 McClelland Boulevard, in 1984.

MISSOURI SOUTHERN STATE COLLEGE

Early in 1937 there was a consensus that a college should be started in Joplin. The board of education, which included E.A. Elliott, school superintendent; Charles Wells; and Cliff K. Titus, worked with a number of citizens, including William Markwardt and Dorothea B. Hoover, to bring this idea to fruition.

That fall Joplin Junior College opened with 114 students and nine faculty members. Classes were conducted by the Extension Division of the University of Missouri in the Joplin High School building at Eighth Street and Wall Avenue.

A bond issue of $50,000 was voted by the city to help finance the college, and in 1938 it moved into a rebuilt former high school building at Fourth Street and Byers Avenue. A full two-year college transfer program was offered.

H.E. Blaine was dean of the college from 1937 to 1947. He is well remembered as "Papa Blaine," who brought his lunch to school in a bucket and stood in the hall every morning to greet each student by name. A faculty contract was worth $1,500, and tuition was sixty dollars per year.

The struggling college weathered World War II. On D-Day, June 6, 1944, classes were dismissed, and the students and faculty went to the old First Community Church to pray with other citizens for their compatriots on the Normandy beaches.

By 1958 enrollment was 626 and the faculty numbered forty-six. The

An aerial view of the main buildings on the Missouri Southern State College campus.

college moved back to the building at Eighth and Wall where there was room for expansion to 1,826 students by 1966.

Changes in the status of the institution were voted in 1964 when a Junior College District was created for Jasper County, ending the twenty-seven years that the college was part of the Joplin Public School System. That year Mission Hills Farm, a large tract of land southwest of the intersection of Newman and Duquesne roads, was suggested as a site for a campus.

Mission Hills Farm had been built by Buck Buchanan, a successful mine operator who also founded the Joplin Stockyards. It was an eleven-room mansion, built in California mission style with cream-stucco walls and red-tile roof.

Following Buchanan's death in 1940, Mr. and Mrs. Frank Wallower bought Mission Hills. The Wallower

A 1984 Missouri Southern State College campus scene in front of Hearnes Hall.

family had been involved in founding the street railway in Joplin, and Frank Wallower had developed a very rich zinc mine in Cardin, Oklahoma, called the Golden Rod, and later mined on Turkey Creek. He later turned to raising cattle at Mission Hills. After his death, Mission Hills was offered for sale.

In 1964 an anonymous donor offered the trustees of Joplin Junior College a gift of $100,000 toward the purchase of Mission Hills. A group of Joplin citizens, led by Morgan Hillhouse, formed the "Friends of the College" committee and raised $305,000. Adding this to the gift, the trustees bought Mission Hills.

The mansion still stands, but the formal gardens, lake, fountain, and orchard had to bow to the exigencies of the new college. The magnificent south view across Turkey Creek remains as impressive as ever. The building is now occupied by the

Business School. Nearby, one of the old barns, with its silo, has been converted into the Barn Theater which the Theater Department still uses.

On April 7, 1964, voters of the Junior College District of Jasper County voted eight to one for a $2.5-million bond issue for the construction of the new campus.

Missouri Southern State College (MSSC) officially came into being in 1965 when House Bill Number 210 was signed by Governor Warren E. Hearnes, who had substantially helped the movement to obtain a four-year college for the Joplin area. A board of regents was appointed to administer the institution. The freshman and sophomore years were funded by the Jasper County Junior College District, and the junior and senior years by the State of Missouri.

In 1967, 2,399 students and ninety-five faculty members enjoyed a beautiful campus, comprised of five new buildings grouped in an attractive crescent, and the enlarged old mansion, under the presidency of Leon C. Billingsly, who served from 1964 to 1978.

The first baccalaureate class of 198 was graduated on June 1, 1969. More than 5,000 students have been graduated since then, and nearly 5,000 have obtained associate degrees.

In 1971 MSSC was granted full accreditation by the North Central Association of Colleges and Secondary Schools, and in 1974 by the National Council of Accreditation for Teacher Education.

In 1977 MSSC became fully state supported. The junior college properties were transferred to the state, while the local levy was retained for debt retirement.

There are now 20 major buildings on 310 acres of countryside, with 4,400 students and 200 faculty members. Dormitories house 550 students. Taylor Performing Arts Center, built in 1974, seats 2,000 and serves both the college and the community. Aca-

The original mansion of the Mission Hills Farm as it appeared in 1965. With additions, it now houses the Business School.

demic studies are pursued in four schools: Arts and Sciences, Business, Technology, and Education and Psychology.

The School of Business has an acknowledged reputation for its highly trained students as well as for its ser-

vice to the business community. The Theater Department's popular children's theater program plays to thousands annually. The Police Academy has gained national recognition. The Education School is a respected source for teachers serving schools throughout southwest Missouri. Science students excel in graduate and professional schools. The Nursing Department, offering both associate and baccalaureate degrees flourishes. The school's athletes, under the team name "The Lions," have gained both state and national fame. Communications students produce weekly programs for MSTV broadcast on local cable. Computer knowledge is integrated into all academic areas.

Dr. Julio Leon, current president, emphasizes that Missouri Southern State College will continue to respond to what is currently happening in the nation and will meet the need for a change from an industrial base to one founded on knowledge and service.

The entrance to Joplin Junior College, at Fourth and Byers streets, which was formerly the local high school building.

EMPIRE DISTRICT ELECTRIC COMPANY

Early Joplinites dearly loved a circus, and in 1880 they were still further delighted by the electric arc lights of Barnum and Bailey's "Greatest Show on Earth."

The city fathers, Oliver Moffett and William G. Sergeant, built a power plant in 1887 for twelve, 2,000-candlepower arc lights, a remarkably early development which occurred only five years after Thomas Edison's discovery.

The following year this plant was incorporated as the Joplin Electric Light and Power Company. In 1890 Moffett moved it to Grand Falls on Shoal Creek, and it was then acquired by the Southwestern Electric Light and Water Power Company. For the first time the plant supplied direct current to electric motors at a Blendville zinc mill.

Another precursor of the Empire Company was founded in 1903 by David D. Hoag and George Moore, who consolidated Southwest Missouri Light Company and Missouri Ice and Cold Storage Company into Consolidated Light Power and Ice Company.

In 1904 Sergeant was back again with Sam and Jamotz Brown to organize the Spring River Power Company, with a dam and hydroelectric plant located in Riverton, Kansas. In 1906 the Spring River Company bought "Old Kate," a 2,000-kilowatt Corliss engine that had supplied power to the 1904 St. Louis World's Fair.

The year 1908 saw electric power supplied to the Joplin and Pittsburgh Railway Company and the Southwest Missouri Railroad Company. As a result, mules no longer pulled the streetcars.

On October 16, 1909, Hoag persuaded Henry L. Doherty to acquire the Joplin Electric Light and Power, Consolidated Light Power and Ice, Joplin Light Power and Water, and the Galena Light and Power companies, which were then consolidated

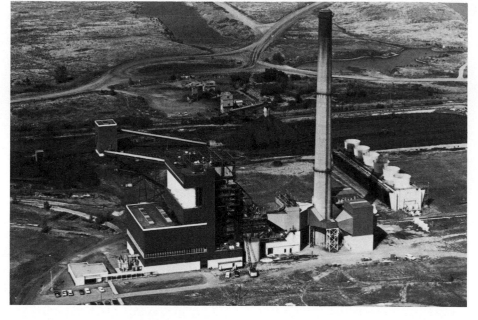

The Asbury plant is Empire District Electric Company's principal generating station.

into the Empire District Electric Company. The area served was known as the Empire Mining District because most of the financing came from New York, the Empire State.

In 1909 the Empire Company had 109 miles of transmission lines, 8,000 kilowatts generating capacity, and 2,364 customers. In 1984 it had 5,700 miles of transmission lines, 622,000 kilowatts generating capacity, and 102,172 customers.

When Empire was formed, electric lighting was expanding from a few of the wealthier homes to all local residences. Domestic consumption increased and has continued to do so. The mines began using electric power, and by the 1920s all had turned to it. But the mines had completely died out by the 1950s, and the large streetcar load had decreased slowly until it ceased completely in 1938. However, this slack has been taken up by a diversified group of light industries that have moved to the Jop-

lin area.

In 1970 Empire built its principal generating station, the Asbury plant. This steam turbine plant is driven by local coal from the Empire Mine of Pittsburgh and Midway Coal Company and generates 192,000 kilowatts. The Empire District Electric Company generates most of its power by coal.

Empire remains dedicated to the people of the district it serves.

In 1906 the Spring River Company bought "Old Kate," a 2,000-kilowatt Corliss engine that had supplied power to the 1904 St. Louis World's Fair. It was housed in this building, which is still standing today.

JONES TRUCK LINES, INC.

In 1918 an eighteen-year-old farm boy, Harvey Jones, started a business in a small way. "I got started when the Missouri-Arkansas Railroad went on strike. We had a farm then and a pair of mules. I hauled wholesale hardware supplies from Rogers to Springdale, Arkansas," says Jones. He used a Springfield wagon hauled by one red mule and one black one. He hauled everything he could get his hands on.

In 1919 Jones made his greatest investment. He sold the wagon and the mules and bought a Federal truck with solid tires. He traveled over the rough local roads hauling mostly lumber and lime.

There were compensations. When at the Springdale railroad station, he met "the prettiest girl I have ever seen." Business prospered, and in 1930 he married that young woman, the former Bernice Young.

The Depression began alleviating in 1933, and Jones changed his firm's name from Jones Transportation Company to Jones Truck Lines, because he had reluctantly decided that mules would not come back into fashion. In 1935 he founded the Jones Truck Lines station in Joplin, which has operated ever since, and after several moves is now located at the intersection of Florida and Newman roads.

By 1936 Jones Truck Lines had added terminals in Fort Smith and Little Rock, Arkansas; Springfield and Kansas City, Missouri; and Tulsa, Oklahoma. The firm owned thirty-three International trucks and constructed a masonry office west of the present one in Springdale. Progress continued with the purchase of routes to St. Louis and Memphis.

During World War II the company's growth slowed, but beginning in 1948 expansion continued apace. Routes were established to Dallas, Texas; Wichita, Kansas; and the Mississippi Delta. Jones Truck Lines was able to break into the Old South

The bright orange Jones Truck Lines' equipment is a familiar sight from Chicago to New Orleans and from Denver to Atlanta.

when that area began to boom. Routes were added to Chicago in 1960 and to Colorado, Georgia, and Alabama by 1976.

Today Jones Truck Lines is a general-commodity common carrier specializing in less-than-truckload shipments. The firm operates from Chicago to New Orleans and from Denver to Atlanta. It owns about 4,000 units, including tractor-trailers, straight trucks, company cars, and forklifts. The company does about $175 million in annual business and employs a total of 2,400 employees.

In 1968 Harvey and Bernice Jones built a church on the shores of the Grand Lake of the Cherokees, near Grove, Oklahoma, and they decided to dedicate the surrounding land to preserve pioneer buildings and arti-

facts. This has grown into the famous Har-Ber Village. Here visitors are welcomed daily, and 375,000 people each year take advantage of this facility.

Current president John Karlberg maintains the owners' record of hard work and a positive attitude, which helps to maintain the excellent service record of Jones Truck Lines, Inc.

After World War II Jones Truck Lines began expanding in earnest. Here Virgil (left) and Gerald Cordes relax by the firm's 1948 International Harvester KB8 trucks.

JONES BROTHERS CONSTRUCTION COMPANY

Albert Jones, co-founder.

His two elder sons, Albert and Hank, were inspired to go into building as their life's work, and in 1923 began their apprenticeship with the M.E. Gillioz Construction Company in Monett, Missouri.

By 1935 they had gained enough experience to found their own partnership, known as the Jones Brothers Construction Company. The pair worked out of Albert's home at 1801 Jackson Avenue. One of the firm's first jobs still stands: the filling station (now a store) at the corner of Seventh Street and Joplin Avenue.

Times were still difficult in 1935, but the worst of the Great Depression was over. In those "good old days" the forty-hour week was little known; workers labored forty-eight hours or not at all. Carpenters made seventy-five cents per hour; painters, sixty-five cents; and common laborers, thirty-five cents. On the other hand, bread was six cents per loaf, coffee was twenty-eight cents per pound, and steak was fifteen cents per pound.

The elder Jones had teamed with William Garrison and then with his younger son, Kenneth, to continue his own construction work, but joined the Jones Brothers firm around 1938 and worked there until his death in 1958. Eugene Stinnett, now vice-president, joined the business in 1935, and his father, Earl Stinnett, came aboard the following year.

Jones Brothers enjoyed the boost of World War II, which allowed for the construction of a portion of Camp Crowder at Neosho, Missouri. In 1944 it handled a relatively large job: construction of the Thurston Chemical Company (now W.R. Grace and Company, Agricultural Chemicals), east of Duenweg, Missouri. Two years later the firm was incorporated.

From then on it handled many large local jobs, including the Junge Bakery, now Safeway Bakery, located

Henry "Hank" Jones, co-founder.

at 1401 Junge Boulevard, in 1947; Vickers, now Sperry Vickers, 2800 West Tenth Street, 1951; the First Christian Church in Neosho, 1960; additions to the Goodrich plant in Miami, Oklahoma, 1964; Mays City, 1416 East Seventh Street, 1965; the Spiva Park, corner of Fourth and Main, 1966; the Joplin Municipal Building, 303 East Third Street, 1966; and St. Mary's Catholic Church, Twenty-fifth Street and Moffet, 1967.

In 1940 Donovan G. Stinnett, Eugene's brother, went to work for the company; he became president in 1970. Albert and Hank Jones were recognized as construction experts in Joplin. Don Stinnett continues their tradition of excellence after more than 14,400 industrial jobs well done.

After James L. Jones married in 1903, he began commercial building and started a family trend that is carried on today by his sons Albert and Henry "Hank." James L. Jones teamed up with A.B. Corey and built principally in Kansas. He lived in Galena, Kansas, at that time a rip-roaring mining town. Jones later joined Bill Garrison and built the high school and gymnasium at Sixth and Chicago in Galena as well as schools in Seneca, Missouri, and Columbus, Kansas.

In 1920 Jones came to Joplin and became minister of the Empire Street Baptist Church. He built the Carthage stone church in 1922. It is still standing and is used as the Sunday School.

THE JOPLIN GLOBE

The Joplin Globe was founded on August 9, 1896, by three printers, Lumley C. McCarn, Frank Tew, and Ozra P. Meloy. It was published on the northeast corner of Second and Main streets.

The founders were ardent supporters of Democrat William Jennings Bryan, the fiery advocate of free coinage of silver. His opponent was William McKinley, who supported the gold standard. McKinley won, but Joplin, then considered a Democratic town, was intensely interested in Bryan, and *The Globe*'s support of Bryan gained it acclaim and circulation.

In 1899 *The Globe* was incorporated as The Joplin Globe Publishing Company with a paid-in capital of $5,000. However, shortly thereafter the three founders sold out to Gilbert Barbee, mine operator, builder, and Democratic politician. Barbee established the firm on Virginia Avenue just north of Fourth Street in a building that now houses the circulation department.

In 1910 Barbee sold out to A.H. Rogers of Carthage, who served as president until his death in 1920. His son, Harrison C. Rogers, was president from 1923 to 1946.

In 1922 *The Globe* purchased *The Joplin News-Herald,* which became *The Globe*'s afternoon paper until it ceased publication in 1970. It had descended from the *Sunday Herald,* founded in 1877. In 1901 it consolidated with the *Daily News* as *The Joplin News-Herald.* It was ably edited for years by A.W. "Kit" Carson, who reported in a humorous vein. *The News-Herald* was crippled by a strike in 1922, which led to its sale to *The Globe.*

After the purchase the morning paper, which had become Republican, became *The Globe,* and the afternoon Democratic paper became *The Herald.* The staff joked that they were Republicans in the morning and Democrats in the evening.

The Joplin Globe Building is located at 117 East Fourth Street.

In 1946 Cowgill Blair, who had been general manager since 1923, became president, and the principal ownership was distributed among the Blair, Fred Hughes, and Rogers families. In 1976 *The Globe* was purchased by Ottaway Newspapers, Inc.

The Ottaway company was founded in 1936 by James H. Ottaway, Sr., who had purchased the Endicott, New York, *Bulletin.* In 1944 the Ottaway group bought the Oneonta, New York, *Star.* Since then it has acquired more than thirty newspapers. In 1970 Ottaway Newspapers became a wholly owned subsidiary of Dow Jones and Company, Inc. Each paper in the group determines its own news coverage and editorial position policies and receives consulting services from Ottaway Newspapers.

In 1968 *The Globe* refurbished its quarters and put up one of the most handsome fronts in Joplin. New offset presses were installed in 1984, and the printing quality of the paper has been markedly improved. Today circulation is more than 43,000, and improvements are being made on a tradition dating back to the beginnings of Joplin.

On the same site today, The Globe *occupied these buildings from the early 1900s until twenty years ago when they were razed to make way for the present facility.*

FREEMAN HOSPITAL

In 1922 John W. Freeman and his wife, Florence, gave their home at 2008 Sergeant Avenue to the Methodist Episcopal Church for a hospital as a memorial to their son, Orley, who died of typhoid fever the previous year. They stipulated that the hospital be open to all classes of patients and to all physicians of all schools of medicine practicing in the state of Missouri.

The articles of association, which were filed by a group of Joplin citizens on October 10, 1922, established a board of trustees and contained a reversionary clause giving final ownership to the Methodist Episcopal Church, St. Louis Diocese. At the same time a bond issue of $180,000 was floated, and on May 26, 1925, a connecting wing to the house was opened with seventy-five beds for an acute-care general hospital.

There was no endowment, and operating money was raised locally with success until the onset of the Great Depression in 1929. The years from then to the early 1930s were very difficult, but somehow Freeman Hospital was kept open.

In 1933 Josephine Yates Tisdell became superintendent. She helped in the founding of the Community Auxiliary of Freeman Hospital. She also succeeded in stabilizing the institution's finances, collected delinquent accounts, persuaded some creditors to cancel their claims, and sold hospital insurance. She took a cut in salary, and all employees gave one month of free work and then worked a number of months without receiving pay. Doctors gave generously of both their services and their equipment.

The Community Auxiliary of Freeman Hospital was started by a group of women working in the Methodist and other churches originally to foster the care of underprivileged children and to assist the hos-

Orley Freeman, whose parents, John W. and Florence Freeman, donated their home and grounds in his honor for the establishment of Freeman Hospital.

pital in any emergency. They used time-honored methods of raising money: sales, shows, feeds, and socials. Over the years this organization purchased much-needed equipment such as a new oxygen tent and a new lighting system for the operating room. They also remodeled X-ray

and therapy rooms, furnished a children's ward, and redecorated. In later years the auxiliary provided a large volunteer staff.

During the lean years of the 1930s a Citizens' Committee of the Chamber of Commerce raised more than $6,000. Hospital board members frequently assessed themselves in order to keep the hospital open.

The World War II years were survived, but problems were experienced due to the organization of the hospital. Generally, early administrators were not trained for their duties. Some were pastors of the Methodist Church with deep human interests but without deep material interests. The board also noticed a lack of involvement from lay members of the church.

Rehabilitation and expansion programs were begun during the administration of Paul Detrick (1953-1958). A local drive in 1954 raised $408,238. In 1957 Detrick obtained a Ford Foundation grant of $295,842, and the auxiliary raised $15,000 by door-to-door solicitation. In 1957 the articles of association were changed so

A beautifully terraced garden entrance was contributed to the hospital by the auxiliary.

that the Methodist Church returned the ownership of the hospital to the trustees.

On December 14, 1958, a new wing was opened, bringing the hospital to a 127-bed capacity. A nursing home was included on the fifth floor, later to be dismantled and become part of the general hospital.

By 1967, even though the institution had increased to 134 beds and had also established an intensive-care unit, it was still crowded. More space was needed, and a parking problem was looming.

In 1972 actor Dennis Weaver, a Joplin native who had achieved fame in the 1960s, kicked off a drive for funds for the new hospital. Twenty acres of land were deeded to the institution by Myron McIntosh. About $7,250,000 was raised in addition to a bond issue of $6,854,000, and construction on a new facility was started at 1102 West Thirty-second Street. The site was on undeveloped land on the edge of an old mined area, but had the rough forested charm of the Ozarks. The building was designed to enhance and blend with the setting and was to be limited to two above-ground floors.

The new Freeman Hospital had 144 beds, employed more than 400 people, and was in full operation on August 30, 1975. Patients had been moved from the old to the new facility using every available suitable carriage, and the first baby, James Ragan, was born that same day. Freeman later became a regional birth center. In 1976 the George A. Spiva Perinatal Unit was dedicated, confirming the institution of regional obstetrical care at Freeman.

Freeman Hospital intensified its strong community involvement through medical education, outpatient care, and various diagnostic and rehabilitative programs. In 1976 the Helen Landreth Rainey Cardiac Treatment Center opened, financed by donations from the Rainey family. It provided diagnosis in cardiology as well as exercise therapy. In 1978 the Tel-Med tape library of health information was opened to the public. Two years later the Rosemary Titus Reynolds Health Education Center was built, using a grant of $250,000 from the C.W. Titus Foundation of Tulsa, Oklahoma. This facility included a medical library, audiovisual equipment, four meeting rooms, and a full-time medical coordinator.

In 1981 a long-range planning survey was begun, and the following year a $14-million expansion and renovation project was accepted. The completion of "Day Surg," a one-day surgery center, was the first phase of the expansion and renovation. It was broken out of the original project and completed first due to a 30-percent increase in outpatient procedures the preceding year. It was (and is) the first and only freestanding facility of its kind in the area. Patients treated in the center return home the day of their operation.

Since then, expansion in space, facilities, and service is proceeding apace. Freeman Hospital will continue to keep abreast of important medical advances and use them to help the city that brought it forth and has sustained it.

Freeman Hospital prior to the 1984 expansion and renovation project.

PATRONS

The following individuals, companies, and organizations have made a valuable commitment to the quality of this publication. Windsor Publications and the Joplin Historical Society gratefully acknowledge their participation in *Joplin: From Mining Town to Urban Center.*

Russell Belden Electric Company*
C.C. Machine, Inc.*
Childress Royalty Co.
Commerce Bank of Joplin*
Continental Imports, Inc.
Dutch Village Motel*
Electric Motor Supply, Inc.*
Empire District Electric Company*
FAG Bearings Corporation*
Financial Federal Savings and Loan
    Association
Freeman Hospital*
Dr. and Mrs. John E. Goff
Howsmon's Office Supply and
    Furniture Company*
Jones Brothers Construction
    Company*
Jones Truck Lines, Inc.*
Joplin Building Material Company*
The Joplin Globe*
Joplin Supply Co.
Mark A. Judge, M.D.
MCI Transporters
Monkem Company*
Midwestern Telephone, Inc.
Missouri Southern State College*
Newman's*
Ozark Memorial Park Cemetery*
H. Lang Rogers
St. John's Regional Medical Center*
Sebastian Equipment Co.
Service Packing Co.
Rolla E. Stephens
Tamko Asphalt Products, Inc.*
Mr. & Mrs. O.M. Walstad

*Partners in Progress of *Joplin: From Mining Town to Urban Center.* The histories of these companies and organizations appear in Chapter 7, beginning on page 97.

SELECTED BIBLIOGRAPHY

BOOKS

Britton, Wiley. *Pioneer Life in Southwest Missouri.* Kansas City: Smith-Grieves Co., 1929.

Broadhead, Garland C. *Report of the Geological Survey of the State of Missouri.* Jefferson City: Regan and Carter, 1874.

Brownlee, Richard S. *Gray Ghosts of the Confederacy: Guerrilla Warfare In the West 1861-1865.* Baton Rouge: Louisiana State University Press, 1958.

Davidson, L.S. *South of Joplin: Story of a Tri-State Diggin's.* New York: W.W. Norton & Company, 1939.

Draper, William R. and Mabel. *Old Grubstake Days in Joplin: The Story of the Pioneers Who Discovered the Largest and Richest Lead and Zinc Mining Field in the World.* Girard: Haldeman-Julius, 1946.

Gibson, Arrell M. *Wilderness Bonanza: The Tri-State District of Missouri, Kansas, and Oklahoma* Norman: University of Oklahoma Press, 1972.

Holibaugh, John R. *The Lead and Zinc Mining Industry of Southwest Missouri and Southeast Kansas.* New York: Scientific Publishing Company, 1895.

Hoofnagle, Ruth Utter. "Historical Development of Joplin." Master's thesis, Kansas State Teachers College, 1950.

Illustrated Historical Atlas of Jasper County Missouri. Joplin: Brink, McDonough and Company, 1876.

Jones, Evelyn. *Tales About Joplin: Short and Tall.* Joplin: Harragan House, 1962.

Joplin Globe staff. *Joplin's First 100 Years: As Recorded in the Pages of the Joplin Mining News, the Joplin News Herald, the Joplin America, the Joplin Tribune, the Joplin Globe.* Joplin: Joplin Globe Publishing Company, 1973.

Kirkman, Kay, and Stinnett, Roger. *Joplin, A Pictorial History.*

Virginia Beach: Donning, 1981.

Leitle, Charles Edward. "Adjustment of a Community From an Exhaustible Resource Base to Other Economic Alternatives. A Case History of Joplin, Missouri." Ph.D. dissertation, University of Arkansas, 1972.

Livingston, Joel T. *A History of Jasper County, Missouri, and Its People.* 2 vols. Chicago: Lewis Publishing Company, 1912.

Livingston, Joseph Thomas. *Joplin, Missouri, the City That "Jack" Built, Some of Its Businesses and Its Beauties: One Hundred and Twenty-Five Scenes in Half Tone, Together With a Concise History From 1838 to 1902 Inclusive.* Joplin: Means Moore, 1902.

Lyons, James. *St. Peter's Diamond Jubilee 1877-1952: Seventy-Five Years of Parish History.* Joplin: St. Peter's Catholic Church, 1952.

Netzeband, William F. "A History of Mining in the Tri-State District of Missouri-Kansas-Oklahoma." Paper presented to the Tri-State Section, American Institute of Mining Engineering, May 20, 1970.

North, F.A., ed. *History of Jasper County, Missouri.* Des Moines: Mills and Company, 1883.

Plat Book of Jasper County Missouri. Philadelphia: Northwest Publishing Company, 1895.

Quisenberry, Bruce. *Joplin: A Historical Reading Lecture.* Mimeographed, n.d.

Rafferty, Milton D. *Historical Atlas of Missouri.* Norman: University of Oklahoma Press, 1982.

Sauer, Carl O. *The Geography of the Ozark Highland of Missouri.* Chicago: University of Chicago Press, 1920. Reprint by Greenwood Press, 1968.

Schoolcraft, Henry R. *A View of the Lead Mines in Missouri.* New York: C. Wiley Company, 1819.

Schoolcraft, Henry R. *Journal of a Tour Into the Interior of Missouri*

and Arkansas. London: Sir Richard Phillips and Company, 1821. Reprinted facsimile, University Microfilms International, 1979.

Schrantz, Ward L. *Jasper County, Missouri In the Civil War.* Carthage: Carthage Press, 1923.

Secretary of State. *Official Manual of the State of Missouri.*

Shaner, Dolph. *Story of Joplin.* New York: Stratford House, 1984.

Stephens, Rolla. *Cats and Frentlemen.* Self-published, 1984.

Swallow, George C. *Geological Report of the Country Along the Line of the Southwestern Branch of the Pacific Railroad, State of Missouri.* St. Louis: George Knapp and Company, 1859.

Williams, Walter. *The State of Missouri: An Autobiography.* Columbia: E.W. Stephens Press, 1904.

JOURNALS AND MAGAZINES

"Eagle-Picher History." *Engineering and Mining Journal* 144(1943):68-79.

Holibaugh, John R. "Early Mining in the Joplin District." *Engineering and Mining Journal* 58(1894):508.

"Imprisoned in a Joplin Mine." *Engineering and Mining Journal* 93(1911): 252.

"The Joplin and Girard Railroad." *Engineering and Mining Journal* 22(1877):328.

"Lead Mining in Southern Missouri." *De Bow's Review* 18(1855):389-91.

INDEX